Innovations
in Annual Giving

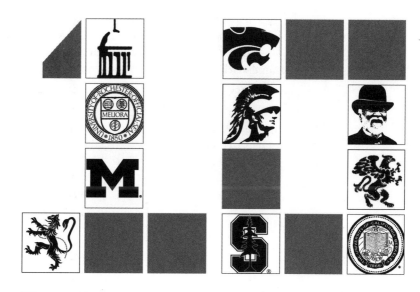

Ten Departures That Worked

By Robert A. Burdenski

University of San Diego

~ University Relations ~ 5998 Alcalá Park ~
~ San Diego ~ CA ~ 92110-2492 ~

ISBN 0-89964-378-7

Printed in the United States of America

The Council for Advancement and Support of Education is the
largest international association of education institutions,
serving more than 3,200 universities, colleges, schools, and
related organizations in 45 countries. CASE is the leading
resource for professional development, information, and standards
in the fields of education fund raising, communications, and
alumni relations.

Art Director: Angela A. Carpenter
Design: Blue Acorn Studio
Editor: Theodore Fischer
Back cover photo courtesy Bentz Whaley Flessner

**COUNCIL FOR ADVANCEMENT
AND SUPPORT OF EDUCATION**®

1307 New York Avenue NW
Suite 1000
Washington DC 20005-4701
www.case.org/books

Table of Contents

To Roger Schifferli,
For thinking of me.

And my wife, Dana,
For thinking with me.

Acknowledgments

Terry Fischer, Deborah Bongiorno, and the staff of CASE Books provided lots of helpful ideas and patience over many months in support of this book. Rachel Pollack and the staff of CASE CURRENTS have also demonstrated great faith in my writing over the years. Their interest and support helped make the idea of a book seem possible in the first place.

A number of people have contributed to my understanding of what good fund raising is all about. They include Alex Petrus, Barbara Patterson, August Napoli Jr., Jim Williamson, Duane Jasper, Edith Falk, Mark Hilton, Frank Huszar, Bruce Flessner, Bobbie Strand, Bill Tippie, and Dr. William Lowery.

Foreword

The year-in, year-out solicitation of unrestricted funds from alumni (and parents and graduating seniors) is often considered to be the unglamorous bedrock of college and university fund raising. Its success, expressed in numbers of dollars raised and percent of alumni who donate, is widely interpreted as a measure of institutional loyalty. For many fund raisers, working for the annual fund is the first step in their careers; from then on status is determined by how swiftly they become "real fund raisers," i.e., major gift officers. Highly susceptible to the environment—the local and national economies, trends in labor markets, traumatic national and international events—and increasingly sophisticated competition from other nonprofits, annual fund raisers keep a sharp eye out for how their peer schools are doing.

Yet, without the fanfare or stewardship opportunities associated with major gifts and capital campaigns, many institutions are content to break even in tough times and incrementally improve when the environment is more favorable.

If these comments seem like an accurate assessment of your institutional experience, then you will find Bob Burdenski's perspective iconoclastic. Bob not only advocates a creative, highly professional approach to annual giving, he also elucidates its conceptional framework and provides real-world examples. Bob celebrates successful practitioners and thoughtfully analyzes the basis of their success. He values long-term strategic planning and stability of leadership. Most profoundly, he understands the role that institutional culture plays but views it as changeable—*and* he provides examples to prove his point. He also argues for the importance of data gathering and data analysis, so that the annual fund can grow beyond frantic efforts "to fill the leaky bucket," to quote one of his favorite terms.

The case studies of 10 annual giving programs in this outstanding book also speak to the importance of top leadership endorsement—whether by the president of Stanford or an Exeter trustee. That leadership sends critical messages to donor constituencies—students/future alumni and existing alumni—that communicate all-important institutional identity.

Moreover, support from the top helps facilitate the removal of internal turf barriers that can create obstacles to effectiveness and efficiency. Successful annual fund operations collaborate with development, capital campaign, alumni relations, student affairs, information services, public relations, and marketing as well as with individual academic units. Only then can they make an effective case for annual giving and effectively brand their appeals as central to the university's mission and goals, thus bolstering in turn the mission of the president or chancellor through a well-designed integrated marketing plan.

Increasingly, widely publicized surveys—most notably, the annual *U.S. News & World Report* study, "America's Best Colleges"—are making competitive benchmarks for alumni participation highly visible. By calling attention to the percentage of (undergraduate) alumni who make annual fund contributions, these surveys have created a powerful categorical imperative across the spectrum of American institutions of higher education: "Thou shalt increase the number of annual giving donors." Pressures on institutional budgets provide an equally strong, nearly universal mandate to increase the amount of current giving.

These case studies provide successful models for meeting these strict objectives and illustrate the importance of tactical goals:

• Securing first-time donors—preferably *before* they graduate

• Retaining existing donors

• Renewing lapsed donors

• Upgrading gifts and increasing donor value

Bob reminds us that exemplary annual giving programs succeed in turning donors into philanthropists identified and primed for major gift cultivation. When these goals are achieved, annual giving attains a position of respect and influence within an institution, and marks a critical difference.

Adrienne A. Rulnick, Ed. D.
Senior Director of Development and Alumni Relations
New York University

Introduction

The great riddle about annual giving goes something like this:

1. Take a program that has a lot of process details, including mailings, student phonathons, e-mail and Web pages, data analysis, market research, and the nurturing of volunteers.

2. Recruit staff persons to learn and manage all these details, hope they don't grow too weary, and pray that no predatory major gift office lures them to a new job outside your campus—or, even more likely, within your campus.

3. Try to keep the program budget funded and hope that war, the economy, anthrax, a campus scandal, or some other unexpected circumstance doesn't waylay your best-laid plans.

Given all of these realities, it's amazing that annual giving occurs at all. It's not a stretch to say that when an annual giving appeal *happens*, it's a victory. When it happens *well*, it's a triumph. And when it somehow implements new strategies that take the program to a whole new level of fund-raising possibility? That's downright *extraordinary*.

A PUZZLED GAZE

For several years now, from visiting with annual giving professionals at colleges, universities, and private schools, I've acquired a pretty good inventory of ideas they've tried in their programs. (Certainly, more than any other species in the world, annual giving directors love to exchange good fund-raising ideas.)

What I've noticed over time, however, is that while the ideas themselves are always valued when shared with other institutions (with CASE, of course, long celebrated as the organization for advancement staff who love to Copy And Steal Everything), just as intriguing is the story of *how* new ideas got implemented at other campuses. Annual giving directors are often befuddled about how to effect such change on their *own* campus. How to get new ideas funded. How to excite the vice president, or the president, or even trustees. How to map out a plan. And how to measure the results.

In appreciation of their confused looks, this book identifies 10 campuses that came up with better ways and explains how they did it.

The annual giving director faces the same treadmill battle as any changing business: Annual giving today bears only a faint familial resemblance to the carbon-paper-and-index-card practices of just 20 years ago. Likewise, this attempt to identify a few of today's cutting-edge programs will undoubtedly look pretty quaint in the not-too-distant future.

A FEW ASSUMPTIONS

In my observation, annual giving programs seek to move prospects along a progression from interested bystander to impassioned philanthropist. My major gift fund-raising friends long ago mapped out a "giving pyramid" that depicts part of that progression. It starts with annual giving at the bottom of the pyramid, with involvement and engagement increasing as donors over time move up the pyramid to capital gifts, endowment gifts, and planned gifts. In the rarefied air atop the pyramid dwell leadership gifts of six or seven (or more) figures. Successful development programs move donors to the top of the pyramid.

While, admittedly, I'm biased, the giving pyramid does not do justice to annual giving programs. Some of the most formidable development challenges shouldered by the annual giving program include:

• Making a compelling case for support that inspires prospects to make their *first* gift, and…

CLASSIC DONOR GIVING PYRAMID

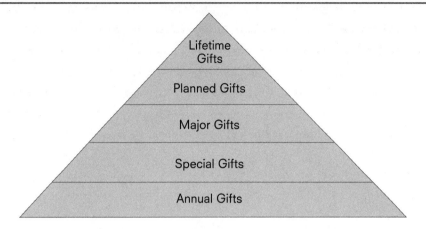

The classic Donor Giving Pyramid rightfully positions annual giving as the foundation for other types of larger gifts. But it fails to acknowledge the stages through which donors progress in the annual giving program itself.

BOB'S ANNUAL GIVING PYRAMID

Bob's Annual Giving Pyramid illustrates how donors progress upward through an annual giving program. An institution inspires feelings of affinity in its donors, teaches a philanthropic culture, and instills a progressively loyal and generous giving habit.

- Identifying from among *supporters* of your institution those who really want to be *philanthropists*.

So, I've taken some annual giving poetic license with the donor pyramid and tailored it to reflect the progression of the annual giving donor. (My major gift friends take comfort in seeing that my pyramid still reaches a pinnacle by identifying major gift prospects, even if they're only *prospects*.)

I believe that the best annual giving programs (10 of which are profiled in this book) all work their way up through the following progression:

- **They promote some kind of ongoing institutional affinity.** Not content to let donors wander in their door (and out again), good annual giving programs create and sustain a relationship with prospect audiences. Most schools enjoy the luxury of having this bond instilled in alumni at graduation. For other types of not-for-profits, forming such relationships is among their hardest tasks. Schools can't take alumni affinity for granted, and alumni apathy is one of the biggest ongoing ailments in annual giving. Many schools use magazines, class notes, reunions, and now Web sites to sustain alumni affinity. It's a critically important component.

- **They introduce an institutional giving culture.** It's easy to suppose that the DNA of alumni of Phillips Exeter Academy (along with Princeton and Wellesley and other schools with *envy-inducing* alumni-giving participation rates) preordains their generosity. In reality, these schools learned long ago the importance of teaching and reinforcing the giving behavior they expect from their alumni. It starts when they're students (sometimes even before they're students) and continues when they're alumni. I visit lots of schools where I'm proudly told that alumni love the place, but that all this affection does not translate into gift support. It doesn't happen by accident.

- **They inspire a first gift.** Whether it's a senior gift program, the pleading of a reunion classmate, a great appeal letter, or a determined student caller, great annual giving programs invariably have great donor acquisition strategies. While oversized seven-figure gifts get all the headlines, for my money the most important step occurs when alumni *first* demonstrate willingness to financially support the school. The leap they take by making their first gift, in terms of distinguishing themselves from other non-donor alumni (and everyone else on the street, for that matter), is enormous.

- **They build donor loyalty.** In 1999, the University of Michigan observed with some anxiety that the majority of their new donors each year were not making second gifts to the university the following year (see Chapter 8). Once an initial gift is received, it is necessary to employ a deliberate set of strategies to build a habit of *annual* gift support.

- **They grow donor value.** It's undeniably valuable to identify an institution's supporters—those individuals who will endorse your work with gifts year after year. But annual giving programs also need to identify prospective *leadership* supporters. President's Circles, Andrew Carnegie Societies, and other giving clubs are valuable only when they motivate alumni to increase giving. Many of your alumni want their annual gifts to make leadership statements. It's up to you to help them.

- **They identify major gift prospects.** I admit it to my major gift friends: The annual giving program shouldn't exist in competition with a major gifts program, but rather in *concert* with it. By identifying long-loyal supporters and leadership annual supporters, the annual giving program serves a critical role in identifying who's really interested in *philanthropy* at your institution. Because many annual giving directors are evaluated only on their program's bottom-line performance, they gnash their teeth each time a donor is "lost" to the major gifts office. The annual giving program should be evaluated—and celebrated—for its role in major gift prospect identification.

While this pyramid progression relates specifically to alumni, it applies equally well to other audiences. Also note that some of these responsibilities lie, in part, outside the annual giving office. It's a shared responsibility that involves the alumni office, the public relations office, advancement services, and other offices.

The 10 programs described in this book all relate to one or more tiers of the annual giving pyramid. While clever annual giving ideas are routinely conceived, copied to death, and ultimately ridden into the ground, I've profiled programs where a good idea had a bigger impact—and actually grew the giving culture or improved the annual giving process.

- Thousands of schools send direct mail, but that doesn't mean they all do it well. When the **University of Iowa** Foundation changed the way it conducted its direct mail appeals on behalf of the colleges of the university, it reminded people of what direct mail should accomplish in the first place.

1. Reed
2. UC Berkeley
3. Stanford
4. USC
5. Michigan
6. Iowa
7. Kansas State
8. Phillips Exeter
9. Rochester
10. Carnegie Mellon

- You wouldn't expect a phonathon to exemplify both cult and culture, but that's what goes on at **Kansas State University**. While comparable-sized universities operate computerized calling centers and hire paid student callers, K-State enjoys steady growth by keeping its old-fashioned phonathon a happening—for students and alumni alike. With more than 2,000 student caller volunteers, the university teaches giving at the same time it asks for gifts.

- The Internet is rapidly changing the way institutions think about annual giving and their relationships with donors. The **University of Rochester** started with a single annual giving Web page and wound up opening a new doorway of enhanced communications with alumni.

- If your alumni-giving participation is less than you'd like it to be, you undoubtedly envy schools that enjoy much higher percentages of support. If you think their alumni are born contributors, you're wrong. **Stanford University** is one school that has been educating students about philanthropy for only a few years—and has watched alumni-giving rates steadily rise over the same period.

- For annual giving programs that have enjoyed some success in growing their alumni-giving participation rate, young alumni often emerge as an obstacle to further growth. **Reed College** decided to embrace young alumni with both arms by forsaking conventional annual giving appeals. With a little help from a lemming, the Reedies show how all marketing is relative—and when you've zigged for a long time it's not a bad idea to zag.

- Plenty of schools command the affection of their alumni, but not every school successfully translates this affection into gift support. Even fewer convert it into volunteer involvement. **Phillips Exeter Academy** has a strong alumni-giving culture and a tradition of volunteer fund-raising leadership that's equally strong—and competitive, too. Schools often resign themselves to the absence of an alumni-giving culture when an investment of businesslike effort in instilling the right behavior can establish a fund-raising tradition.

- Any annual giving program would be happy to attract a large number of $1,000 donors, but donors must be motivated to increase their giving capacity and donate even larger gifts. **Carnegie Mellon University** did it with a scholarship-giving program that inspired $1,000 donors to increase their gifts by introducing them to life as university benefactors.

- Many annual giving programs that do a good job of conducting appeals lack the data necessary to evaluate their results. Without adequate gift reports and good data, it's hard to know where and how to improve. By looking at its donor retention rates, the **University of Michigan** discovered a significant opportunity to increase its donor base and upgrade the value of its donor acquisition appeals.

- In annual giving, we're often guilty of assuming that giving arguments that work for one school will be equally compelling at another. That is, if a letter is successful at your school, that's reason enough to believe that it will be successful at mine. The **University of California, Berkeley** is one program that decided to actually test various reasons for giving and find out how they resonated with Cal alumni.

- Annual giving programs have a whole lot of process involved, from bulk mailings to recruiting students for the phonathon. It's a rare program that can carve out time for program planning and even more unusual to find programs that look several years ahead. The strategic planning process at the **University of**

Southern California serves as a great model for surveying the environment of your annual giving program and planning ahead—even when you don't have the time to do it.

A word of caution. Each of the ideas presented here produced proven growth for the school's annual giving program. Our 10 institutions are recognized, in part, for understanding the right ideas, at the right time, for *their* alumni, *their* program, and *their* institution. A Lemming Society (or any other rodent-like society, for that matter) may simply not be appropriate for your audience. The more you understand its particular dynamics, the more likely you'll energize *your* program.

As I write this, the next wave of change is already underway. Annual giving programs are testing new uses of the Internet, e-mail, and multimedia for communicating the case for support, along with new methods of learning and retaining information about donor interests and motivations. Several school examples that would have been noteworthy additions to this book could not be added—they're still being designed and implemented. I will keep them in mind for next time, because we will all need to keep getting better.

—Robert A. Burdenski

They Created Better Appeals

New Deliveries for Direct Mail

The University of Iowa Foundation embraces a mailing philosophy:
It's direct mail first—and nothing else second

For most colleges and universities, direct mail remains an important component of the annual giving program. Feared near death in the 1990s (and shunned during the anthrax scares of 2001) direct mail has nonetheless enjoyed a bit of a renaissance as fund raisers again appreciate how it gets their appeal seen and read by their prospects. In an increasingly multimedia phone-ringing message-saturated world, direct mail remains a proven method for getting the case for support into people's hands.

But continued use of direct mail does not guarantee that it's being done well. For large institutions as well as small ones, a number of competing factors can impinge upon and compromise the fund-raising prowess of direct mail solicitations:

• The look needs to be consistent with institutional style guidelines and standards.

• The dean wants to personally write the letter.

• The development office needs to piggyback an events calendar and other bits of information.

Sound familiar? These are just a few examples of factors that can wither your direct mail message.

For any single school, these intrusions make direct mail daunting enough. For a central university program that facilitates mailings for many schools and units, the task could easily be terrifying. The University of Iowa took the bull by the horns.

IOWA AT A GLANCE:

UNIVERSITY OF IOWA Iowa City, Iowa	
Nickname	Hawkeyes
Type of institution	Public doctoral/ research university
Founded	1847
Total enrollment	28,768
Endowment market value	$657 million
Total alumni giving for current operations	$13,021,722
Undergraduate alumni of record	118,043
Graduate alumni of record	81,146
Alumni solicited	113,864
Alumni donors	33,601
Participation (of alumni solicited)	30%
Web site	www.uiowa.edu

Kris Meyer serves as the director of annual programs for the University of Iowa Foundation. Following a career in advertising, she arrived at UI in 1997 and set among her initial challenges improving the foundation's direct mail annual giving appeals on behalf of the entire university.

The foundation's central annual giving program had tried mightily to cater to what various academic units thought they needed their direct mail to look like and accomplish. In the crush to produce mailings on a dozen different types of letterhead, though, Meyer needed to determine whether the central office was producing *effective* direct mail.

"What I found when I arrived was typical of direct mail found at most universities," said Meyer. "The letters were no more than departmental newsletters with occasional solicitations buried within the text—if you could convince the letter signer to be bold and actually ask for a gift. A specified dollar amount in a gift ask was rare. No P.S. was ever used. No teaser copy on envelopes to get people to open the letter either."

As at many schools, direct mail at UI had become defined in different ways by the various units (or, as Meyer refers to them, "clients") served by the central annual giving staff. (Annual giving offices of all sizes will identify with the experience of "hijacked" appeals that often wind up communicating message points very different from the ones with which they start out.)

Meyer saw a red flag. "The clients were saying. 'This is the only time that people are going to hear from us this year.' The mailings read like newsletters and had little emotion. They had a consistent institutional look, but were consistently *not* focused on any fund-raising objectives. People have to commit to the goal of the appeal letter itself. The goal is to raise money and increase alumni participation. Clients should have been separately sending a newsletter or a dean's update letter."

Easy enough to say, but shooing deans, development officers, even presidents out of the direct mail kitchen is easier said than done. The critical moment, obviously, came when Meyer needed to convince her clients to let the annual giving office handle the job. Meyer was grateful for the open-mindedness of many of her deans and department heads.

CHANGING THE CULTURE

"When we first started, we were just trying to include some basic direct marketing tactics in the letters: highlight portions of the text by underlining, add a P.S. And many clients began to have success with more aggressive fund-raising letters," said Meyer.

Pointing out successful examples comforted doubtful clients. "The UI Department of Physics and Astronomy had been successfully fund raising by mail for some time," said Meyer. "We suggested some intriguing lead copy ideas for the beginning of their letter. They trusted us and we did it. They had good success. That enabled me to go to other deans and units and point to the examples."

Once the shift in copy and design began, Meyer kept preaching strategy. It was important to educate her internal audience about maintaining a marketing focus—as distasteful as that seemed to some. "We talked about direct marketing tactics. 'Tactics' is such a negative word—but we're not writing a social letter, we're writing a direct mail solicitation. We're not just competing with other charities; we're also competing with other mail. The biggest and first challenge we face

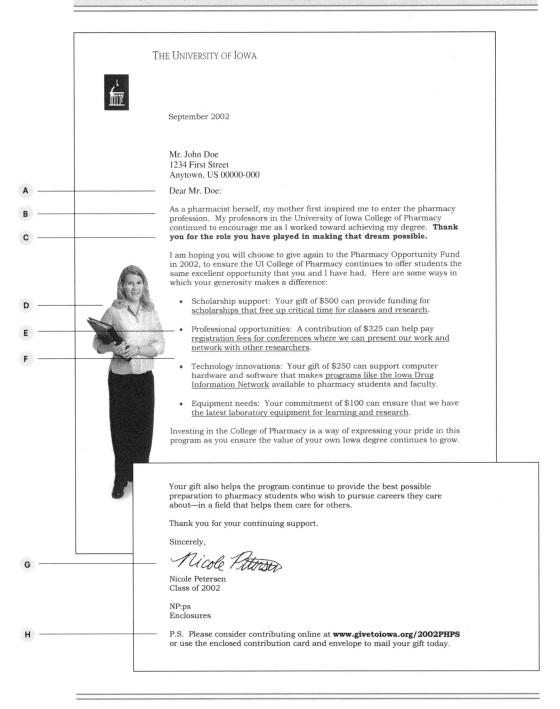

THE UNIVERSITY OF IOWA

September 2002

Mr. John Doe
1234 First Street
Anytown, US 00000-000

A — Dear Mr. Doe:

B — As a pharmacist herself, my mother first inspired me to enter the pharmacy
profession. My professors in the University of Iowa College of Pharmacy
continued to encourage me as I worked toward achieving my degree. **Thank**
C — **you for the role you have played in making that dream possible.**

I am hoping you will choose to give again to the Pharmacy Opportunity Fund
in 2002, to ensure the UI College of Pharmacy continues to offer students the
same excellent opportunity that you and I have had. Here are some ways in
which your generosity makes a difference:

D — • Scholarship support: Your gift of $500 can provide funding for
scholarships that free up critical time for classes and research.

E — • Professional opportunities: A contribution of $325 can help pay
registration fees for conferences where we can present our work and
network with other researchers.

F — • Technology innovations: Your gift of $250 can support computer
hardware and software that makes programs like the Iowa Drug
Information Network available to pharmacy students and faculty.

• Equipment needs: Your commitment of $100 can ensure that we have
the latest laboratory equipment for learning and research.

Investing in the College of Pharmacy is a way of expressing your pride in this
program as you ensure the value of your own Iowa degree continues to grow.

Your gift also helps the program continue to provide the best possible
preparation to pharmacy students who wish to pursue careers they care
about—in a field that helps them care for others.

Thank you for your continuing support.

Sincerely,

Nicole Petersen

G — Nicole Petersen
Class of 2002

NP:ps
Enclosures

H — P.S. Please consider contributing online at **www.givetoiowa.org/2002PHPS**
or use the enclosed contribution card and envelope to mail your gift today.

A. Salutation: We feel it's important to personalize letters, especially when we're mailing to previous donors. It sends a message that we have a relationship with them.

B. Lead: We want the lead to catch their attention. The first two sentences are there to answer the questions, "Why are they writing to me?" and "Why should I keep reading?"

C. Thank You: We always want our previous donors to know that their gifts are appreciated. We don't want them to feel like they're being lumped in with the masses. We want them to feel a little special.

D. Photo: People digest a letter visually, just as much as they do by reading it in text order, so the photo is an important affirmation of several things. A student is writing to them personally. They are supporting individual people, not the institution. This letter was useful because it was designed to appeal to both older and younger alumni. Younger alumni related to the student's experience, and the older alumni were more likely to relate to it as parents. Just like the lead, a good visual can help catch someone's attention and hold it.

E. Bullet Points: Bullet points are another good visual technique. They let us break text into several critical messages. If you could only pull out a few thoughts, what would they be? Because that's all they will read.

F. Suggested Gift Amounts: Histograms come into play here, since they suggest a range of gifts based upon median gift sizes for each mailing segment. By suggesting examples of how gifts are used, it allows prospective donors to see the impact of each individual gift—adding meaning to the reason to give.

G. Signature: With all the mail we send, we don't have the ability to personally sign each piece—but it's another opportunity to add a personalized touch. Using a student and listing her graduation year is more appealing than the more institutional voice of the dean or the annual giving director.

H. P.S.: The P.S. remains a proven visual "destination." People read them. We're now using them to promote online giving, and we use a variety of Web address codes so that we can track the effectiveness of each mailing and how many people it brings to the Web giving page.

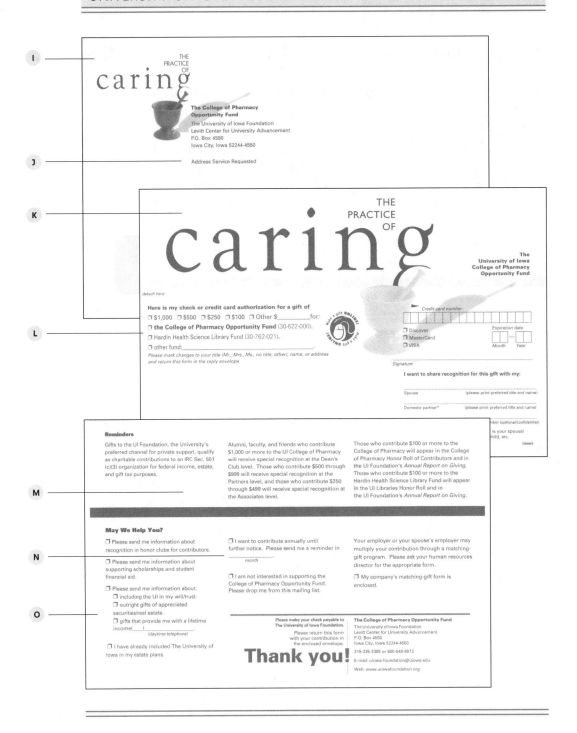

THE
PRACTICE
OF

caring

**The College of Pharmacy
Opportunity Fund**

The University of Iowa Foundation
Levitt Center for University Advancement
P.O. Box 4550
Iowa City, Iowa 52244-4550

Address Service Requested

THE
PRACTICE
OF

caring

The
University of Iowa
College of Pharmacy
Opportunity Fund

detach here

Here is my check or credit card authorization for a gift of

❏ $1,000   ❏ $500   ❏ $250   ❏ $100   ❏ Other $_____ for:

❏ **the College of Pharmacy Opportunity Fund** (30-622-000).

❏ Hardin Health Science Library Fund (30-762-021).

❏ other fund:_____

*Please mark changes to your title (Mr., Mrs., Ms., no title, other), name, or address
and return this form in the reply envelope.*

Credit card number

❏ Discover
❏ MasterCard
❏ VISA

Expiration date

Month   Year

Signature

I want to share recognition for this gift with my:

Spouse   (please print preferred title and name)

Domestic partner*   (please print preferred title and name)

...ber (optional/confidential)
...is your spousal
...hild, etc.   (over)

Reminders

Gifts to the UI Foundation, the University's preferred channel for private support, qualify as charitable contributions to an IRC Sec. 501 (c)(3) organization for federal income, estate, and gift tax purposes.

Alumni, faculty, and friends who contribute $1,000 or more to the UI College of Pharmacy will receive special recognition at the Dean's Club level. Those who contribute $500 through $999 will receive special recognition at the Partners level, and those who contribute $250 through $499 will receive special recognition at the Associates level.

Those who contribute $100 or more to the College of Pharmacy will appear in the College of Pharmacy Honor Roll of Contributors and in the UI Foundation's *Annual Report on Giving.* Those who contribute $100 or more to the Hardin Health Science Library Fund will appear in the UI Libraries Honor Roll and in the UI Foundation's *Annual Report on Giving.*

May We Help You?

❏ Please send me information about recognition in honor clubs for contributors.

❏ Please send me information about supporting scholarships and student financial aid.

❏ Please send me information about:
   ❏ including the UI in my will/trust.
   ❏ outright gifts of appreciated securities/real estate.
   ❏ gifts that provide me with a lifetime income(____).
   _____
   (daytime telephone)

❏ I have already included The University of Iowa in my estate plans.

❏ I want to contribute annually until further notice. Please send me a reminder in
_____
month

❏ I am not interested in supporting the College of Pharmacy Opportunity Fund. Please drop me from this mailing list.

Your employer or your spouse's employer may multiply your contribution through a matching-gift program. Please ask your human resources director for the appropriate form.

❏ My company's matching-gift form is enclosed.

Please make your check payable to
The University of Iowa Foundation.
Please return this form
with your contribution in
the enclosed envelope.

Thank you!

The College of Pharmacy Opportunity Fund
The University of Iowa Foundation
Levitt Center for University Advancement
P.O. Box 4550
Iowa City, Iowa 52244-4550

319-335-3305 or 800-648-6973

E-mail: uiowa-foundation@uiowa.edu

Web: www.uiowafoundation.org

I. Outside Envelope: The outside package has two jobs: get into the hands of the prospect and get opened. So it needs to get where it's going and it needs to be compelling enough to motivate someone to open it. We like using a different size package (6 x 9), and we try to feature a visual, so that it gets to the top of their mail pile.

J. Address Updating: We try to mail people frequently enough so that our addresses stay accurate, but we'll use postal services to keep up-to-date as well. If you're not constantly working to keep your database accurate, you're literally throwing money away.

K. Contribution Card: Because our mailings don't solicit pledges—just outright gifts—we don't call them "pledge cards."

L. Suggested Gift Amounts: We typically suggest a range that motivates people to give more than they might otherwise (lowest number) while also sending the message that people give larger amounts as well (highest number). If they're looking at the card at this point, they've probably decided they want to be supporters, so this helps define that for them by suggesting a gift range.

M. Donor Recognition: We've set a minimum giving level for annual report recognition as a way of motivating our donors to give at least $100. It also helps manage the costs of producing the annual report, since it reduces the size of the published donor list.

N. Recurrent Giving: We've started to invite people to tell us if they want to automatically make their gifts again in the future. Recurrent giving via credit cards and electronic funds transfer will increasingly be part of our appeals. I think we've oversold annual giving—we've taught our donors to make a single gift each year. Many would make gifts more frequently if we promoted that option.

O. Suggested Giving Destination: The goal is to raise unrestricted funds for our client units. So while we offer donors the ability to write in other gift destinations, we don't encourage them. We've found that several of our units have alumni that respond to supporting the library.

is getting our envelopes opened. So, we began to put strategic teaser copy on the outside envelope."

Predictably enough, questions were raised about reconciling "teaser copy" with the "institutional look." How does Meyer balance institutional style with the need to have her appeal mail opened? "I don't think you have to be wild; you just have to get noticed. And getting noticed doesn't have to be an offensive thing. It can be very classy," she said. "There's a prestige to fund raising for higher education that we absolutely respect. The neon-orange envelope and the urgent fake overnight packaging aren't things we would do. Some of the tactics that would work for broader audiences would never work for the University of Iowa."

Meyer examines other annual giving programs and occasionally smells fear. "They're hesitant to be remarkable. Or they can't think of a way to make themselves appear remarkable because they look at their work in the same way every day. Our staff works hard to seek out the remarkable things that go on at the university, and our editorial staff is truly psyched to write about them. I simply encourage them to make sure that emotion comes through in our mailings."

HOLD THEIR ATTENTION

Once she and the foundation's creative staff redesigned the outside of appeals, Meyer turned her attention to the messages inside. Getting the envelope opened is just the beginning of the battle.

"We need to engage our readers in the first few seconds. 'Hello, I'm the dean of so-and-so college…' just *doesn't* have any emotion," said Meyer. "You need an emotional appeal to get the reader's attention and get them to read. We are a research institution, and we talk about how research has impacted lives, rather than just the laboratory itself. We tie it back to how private gift dollars are making remarkable things possible."

Meyer considers a mailing's lead, or opening sentences, to be *sacred*. All the work that has gone into getting a letter into prospects' hands and getting them to open it goes for naught if they don't transmit the main message points.

A good visual image can help. A direct mail letter for the College of Pharmacy that featured a prominent picture of a student "pulled" (generated gift responses) significantly higher than previous traditional letter efforts.

"We wanted to emphasize the benefit that every student receives from annual gift support of the college, so featuring a single student was more compelling than a building or a dean." The picture was complemented by a first-person letter written by the student herself. (See the full text letter on page 14.)

ADVICE FOR SMALLER SCHOOLS

With an in-house creative staff that services the entire development operation, Meyer admits to possessing resource luxuries many institutions lack. She also believes that one strength of the UI program is the annual giving staff's ability to provide direct marketing expertise to its clients—including data analysis.

"We conduct a lot of statistical analysis. We use Target Analysis Group donorCentrics™ Strategic analytical management reports to review what happened last year with our clients and discuss the specific giving characteristics of their donors," said Meyer. "Are they increasing their gifts, are they being retained from year to year? It's a very compelling discussion. We then try to come up with some new angles. Will this year's piece have a gift upgrade emphasis? What was the average gift generated for their audience last year? We know if they need to be more participation-oriented or upgrade-oriented. If participation is an issue, then we need to send a message that's different from what we'd say to an audience that has good participation but a stagnant average gift amount. If we've done our homework and we have an understanding of the giving situation, we'll design a piece that will likely achieve some new goals, satisfy the client, and keep overall alumni participation on the rise."

For institutions of all sizes, regardless of their resources, here's what Meyer suggests:

- **Figure out what you want to do best and do it**. If you want your mailings to be a solicitation and a newsletter and a letter from the president, you'll probably dilute all of those messages. Don't assume you have to load it up with stuff, as if the next mailing is the only train going to a destination. Don't give in. Rely on direct marketing experience.

- **Develop your own benchmarks**. You don't need an elaborate statistical model. Decide on a few benchmarks and measure them each year according to the same methodology. Meyer recommends knowing overall retention rate, average gift, and median gift for your total donor base as well as three key segments:

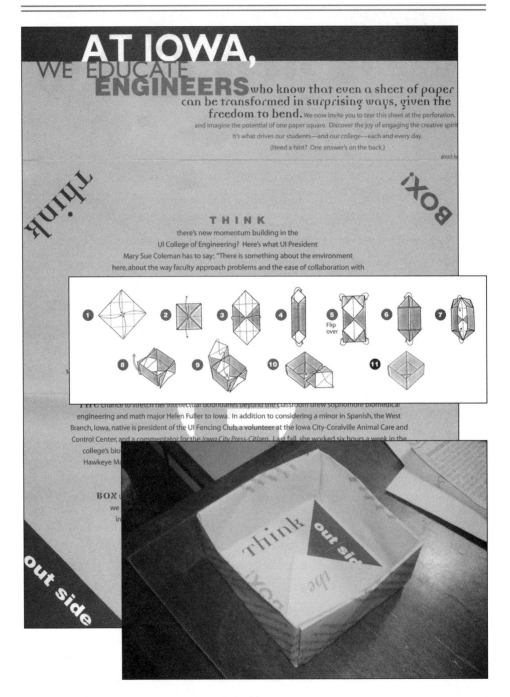

AT IOWA,

WE EDUCATE

ENGINEERS who know that even a sheet of paper can be transformed in surprising ways, given the freedom to bend. We now invite you to tear this sheet at the perforation, and imagine the potential of one paper square. Discover the joy of engaging the creative spirit. It's what drives our students—and our college—each and every day.

(Need a hint? One answer's on the back.)

detach here

THINK
there's new momentum building in the
UI College of Engineering? Here's what UI President
Mary Sue Coleman has to say: "There is something about the environment
here, about the way faculty approach problems and the ease of collaboration with

THE chance to stretch her intellectual boundaries beyond the classroom drew sophomore biomedical engineering and math major Helen Fuller to Iowa. In addition to considering a minor in Spanish, the West Branch, Iowa, native is president of the UI Fencing Club, a volunteer at the Iowa City-Coralville Animal Care and Control Center, and a commentator for the *Iowa City Press-Citizen*. Last fall, she worked six hours a week in the college's bio...
Hawkeye Ma...

BOX ...
we ...
in ...

An Iowa appeal to engineering alumni ingeniously captures their attention by folding into a box.

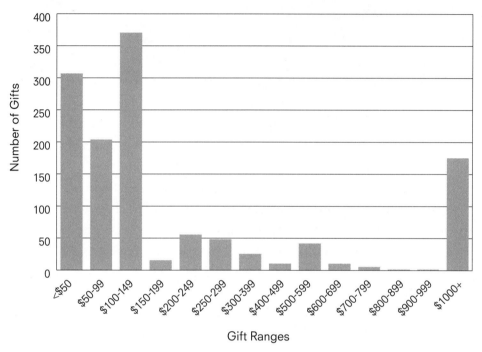

Gift Ranges

Histograms identify the giving levels where Iowa donors congregate. The unit above, with a large number of supporters at lower giving levels ($149 or less), needs to do a better job of growing donor value by increasing gift amounts.

new donors, LYBUNTs (last year but not this year), and SYBUNTs (some years but not this year). Meyer is a big fan of histograms, which show how numbers of donor gifts break out across a range of gift sizes. "We don't know how to upgrade people if we can't see the dollar levels where donors are clustering. If everyone is giving at $250, then I'd suggest thinking about what will get them to $300 or $500. Don't just keep generating the same results because 'that's the way it's always been done.'" Track data that will help you evaluate and refine your appeals.

• **Learn from others.** "Every few years, I send 10 gifts to 10 different charities and that usually gets me all the direct mail they send out," said Meyer. "Then, we keep a direct mail file. We are able to look at the teaser copy, the size of the piece, the use of metering or stamps. Right now I am very interested in learning how nonprofits are using automation, and how they are increasing cost-effectiveness." Increasingly, she looks at how organizations are integrating direct mail and the Internet in appeals.

Ask Meyer to cite her most important principles in direct mail and you get a series of rapid-fire answers: "I want a great lead—the letter has to grab the reader's attention. I want a P.S., because it's proven research that the reader's eye will gravitate to it every time. I want creative ask amounts with bullet points and visual breaks—we need to guide the reader's eye down the page. I want a gift ask in the first paragraph or two, with a minimum of three asks in every letter. We're trying to get a gift, and we shouldn't be too indirect about it."

Meyer is bullish about the future of direct mail at the University of Iowa. "We've gotten direct mail to a point where I'm very excited about what's coming next. We have statistics to measure results, and we've gotten our benchmarking to a point where I'm really very excited. We're integrating new technologies as well. Our direct mail will increasingly reference our Web content and will lead our audiences to our Web site."

The changes will be the latest in a series for a program that could have stuck to its longstanding structures. As a result of some thoughtful changes, Meyer has enjoyed the results that come from daring to be different. "We had clients who hated our approach, but most understood the strategy. We proved that it works. We have a job to do. We do it differently and we do it well."

Kris Meyer's persistence in adjusting the direct mail culture at the University of Iowa is a reminder that direct mail communicates the same way as radio and television commercials or billboards. To build the giving culture with alumni and other constituents, you must get message points across with consistency and with some regularity. This requires more than putting mail in the mail. It requires a coordinated production process, a clever attention-getting look (which can vary for each prospect audience), careful construction of the inside materials, and the ability to review and evaluate the effectiveness of what you've done.

Allow your direct mail to be direct mail.

Images of children generate direct mail gifts for many types of charitable organizations, including the University of Iowa.

MAILING TO NON-DONORS?
THE UNIVERSITY OF SASKATCHEWAN ROCKS WITH THE '60S

The University of Iowa does not use its direct mail program to acquire donors; instead, mailings are part of a strategy for renewing and reactivating previous donors. When colleges and universities seek to cut costs and reduce the number of low-return mailings, the question gets asked: "Should we solicit our non-donor alumni every year?"

The University of Saskatchewan annual fund program solicits 25,000 alumni each year by telephone and mail. While the U of S actually claims thousands more alumni, resource limitations have forced the annual giving program to make tough decisions about prioritizing its prospect audiences. Since solicitations of previous donors produce the greatest returns on calls and mailings, should the university forsake its non-donor population to maximize revenues today?

The U of S annual giving staff decided to adopt a rotating decade-based approach for its non-donor audience. While many institutions use a similar approach to segment non-donor alumni, the U of S included an additional focus: The annual fund staff would solicit only those non-donors who graduated in a specific decade—in this case, the 1960s. And to do it they designed a customized appeal that went beyond simple decade-specific telemarketing script references or letter copy.

The annual giving staff chose a "'60s Campus Rally" theme to create "event" excitement that could be repeated in subsequent years with audiences from other decades. A well-known '60s graduate serving as the chairperson added enthusiasm to the appeal.

To combine feelings of nostalgia with an effective case for support, they assembled a brochure that had the look and feel of the '60s. Outside, it featured an old yearbook photo of a group of students captioned: "In the '60s, you criticized the apathy of the middle class." The brochure opened to reveal a photo of current students in similar pose with the caption: "We have a few students who would like to hear from you." (See page 28.) Lyrics from '60s-era songs reinforced the theme, and the mailing included a personal letter from the appeal chair that invoked additional campus memories and added some useful peer pressure.

"In discussing the appeal with the chair, we sought to give the '60s alumni the feeling that we really did have an appreciation for what times were like when they went to school," said Elaine Cadell, the U of S executive director of alumni and development. "The chair himself noted the irony that the apathy that we protested as students was now afflicting many of his classmates. He encouraged us to take the tongue-in-cheek approach with it that we did."

The strategy paid off. The mailing generated an 8 percent participation rate and an average gift of $53, strong numbers for a longtime non-donor audience and a figure that exceeded the announced goals. More than 400 first-time donors were attracted from a long-time nonparticipating group, and the $21,000 raised was twice the appeal's cost—a healthy 50-cent cost-of-raising-a-new-dollar.

Equally gratifying were the comments of many '60s prospects. "We received many positive responses from alumni. They thanked us for remembering the era, and a few even recalled the photo itself," said Cadell.

The U of S annual giving staff sustained the '60s theme in thanking new donors. "We went to a local old record shop and made a deal for a lot of old 45 rpm records. (If you don't know what these are, ask your vice president)," said Cadell. The records were sent in clear plastic sleeves with an acknowledgement card from the appeal chair noting, "You've made me so very happy." (A benediction from Blood, Sweat, and Tears, if you will.) (See page 29.)

"I really think it worked for us because we gave these alumni a fresh look and an appeal that they could personally identify with," concluded Cadell. "Instead of treating all non-donors the same, or not communicating with them at all, we focused on a subset of them—and they responded."

May, 1999

Mr. U. R. Alumni
123 Giving Way
Saskatoon, SK S7N 5C8

Dear Mr. Alumni:

"All You Need is Love"

. . . or so it seemed in the '60s. It was a great decade, a time when university students everywhere heightened their sense of social responsibility, optimism and global understanding.

I look back with fond memories of my own student experience — the activities I was involved in, the people whom I befriended, and the many lessons I learned during those years. I'm sure you also have good memories of your time here. But things have changed since you and I went to university. More than a decade of funding cutbacks and "making do with what we've got" is taking its toll today.

I'm asking you to help me revive the "helping our fellow man" spirit so typical of our era by taking part in the **'60s Campus Rally** — an effort by graduates of the 1960s to alleviate the serious situation now facing U of S students.

Without more library resources, updated equipment, scholarships and bursaries, our students will not receive the same level of education enjoyed by those that graduated before them. In fact, unless more scholarships, bursaries and student aid are made available, some students will not be able to attend university at all.

Why am I asking you to get involved? Like you, many '60s grads have yet to support their alma mater. But, we know there is great potential for giving. I'm hoping that your own university experience has led to your success since graduation, and that your success will be reflected in your commitment to the young people of the '90s.

For this reason, I want you to consider a gift of $60 to the **'60s Campus Rally**. Please take the time to contemplate your gift carefully. It's up to us – you and me – to create a legacy for U of S students. I can assure you that all gifts, of all sizes, are sincerely appreciated and needed.

Alumni and Development, University of Saskatchewan
Second Floor Kirk Hall, 117 Science Place, Saskatoon SK S7N 5C8 Telephone: (306) 966-5186 Facsimile: (306) 966-5571

Send generic direct mail to all non-donors or focus on a targeted audience?
The University of Saskatchewan focused on the '60s.

What you give today will help us develop the leaders of tomorrow, in a wide range of disciplines, throughout the world. You will also help preserve the standards of excellence that have remained the hallmark of a degree from the University of Saskatchewan. It is up to us to meet the challenge of inadequate funding, to pick up where others have left off.

I urge you to take the time today to make your gift. You can give right this moment by calling toll-free 1-888-293-1907 (24 hours/day), or by using our secure online gift option at http://www.usask.ca.alumni/fundraising/annualfund. Or, you can send your cheque or money order along with the donor card at the bottom of this letter. The choice is yours.

On behalf of the students and your University, thank you for taking up a good cause. And, of course, many thanks for your support.

Regards,

Russ Kisby

Russ Kisby, Class of '63
Honorary Spokesperson, **'60s Campus Rally**

P.S. Now is the time to "rally" around University of Saskatchewan students! As a fellow 1960s graduate, please join me in the **'60s Campus Rally**.

An appeal letter, signed by a Class of '63 alumnus and loaded with lyrical references to '60s songs, sent the message that the appeal targeted alumni of that era.

In the '60s, you criticized the apathy of the middle class.

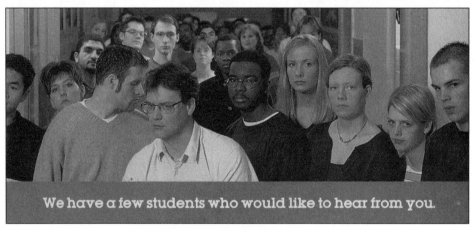

We have a few students who would like to hear from you.

The U of S restaged a '60s photo with today's students to make a connection — and a case for gift support — to '60s-era alumni.

"You've made me so...very happy!"

Blood, Sweat and Tears, 1969

Thank you for supporting the '60s Campus Rally! Your gift will enhance the education of students, and continue the legacy of caring that is the hallmark of our University of Saskatchewan.

"For the record", here's a small memento of those bygone days when the 45 was king. Your gift was music to our ears!

We hope you will always feel part of our University. We look forward to your future interest, involvement and support.

Russ Kisby, Class of '63
Honorary Spokesperson
1999 Annual Fund

To acknowledge gifts, the U of S sent actual 45 rpm records.

A Volunteer Phonathon for the Ages

In an era when computerized calling centers and hired students are presumed indispensable, the K-State paper-pledge-card-and-volunteer-based program raises eyebrows—and millions of dollars

t takes a moment for it to dawn on you. The scene in Manhattan, Kansas, at the annual Kansas State University phonathon at first seems like an anachronism, as if you have stepped into a circa 1979 annual fund drive. Students hunch over pledge cards, phones cradled in the crooks of their necks while they scribble down contact updates, questions, and thank-you notes. The K-State annual fund phonathon is a throwback that seems to have bypassed automation and paychecks for student callers. With a troop of student volunteers armed only with pledge cards and telephones, what hasn't been forgotten is how to raise money. A lot of money.

"Phonathon innovation" might describe new telemarketing sorftware that automatically weeds out busy signals, answering machines, and underperforming student callers. Not at Kansas State. For institutions that face limitations on automation and other resources, or are simply looking for a good profitable time, the K-State program is a role model. Sometimes the smartest program decisions are the changes you *don't* make. K-State proves that phonathons run the old-fashioned way can still succeed.

In the 1980s and 1990s, as other campuses installed computerized calling systems, K-State continued to maximize its main resource: a legion of volunteers. It was a deliberate decision. "It's not that we didn't have the resources," said Gordon Dowell, director of the annual giving program. "If anything, I've had to

KANSAS STATE AT A GLANCE:

KANSAS STATE UNIVERSITY Manhattan, Kansas	
Nickname	Wildcats
Type of institution	Public doctoral/ research university
Founded	1863
Total enrollment	19,417
Endowment market value	$235 million
Total alumni giving for current operations	$8,970,828
Undergraduate alumni of record	104,652
Graduate alumni of record	33,565
Alumni solicited	122,138
Alumni donors	32,603
Participation (of alumni solicited)	27%
Web site	www.ksu.edu

defend why we weren't following along with other peer institutions. We were conspicuous because we kept doing things the same way, but the results have validated the approach and made believers of the skeptical."

NIGHT FALLS ON MANHATTAN

For a little over a month during the dead of winter, at a bit before six o'clock on Sunday through Thursday nights, students from all over campus begin crowding into the Hollis Telefund Center for training. Thirty minutes later they are unleashed on the phones, critical participants in the world's largest all-volunteer telephone campaign for higher education. Sitting at more than 80 calling stations for the next three and a half hours, K-State students become the means by which alumni make an annual reunion with the alma mater.

During over 21 calling session nights in February 2000, the K-State program involved more than 1,400 students, received more than 21,000 pledges, and raised more than $1.2 million. Pledge records were broken in each of the university's nine colleges, as were records for total alumni donors and overall pledge totals. Since the program's inception, in 1979, volunteers have solicited more than 320,000 pledges totaling more than $13 million. This has been done the same way for more than 20 years: without a single headset, computer terminal, or paid caller. Because of low overhead and a unique tradition of alumni giving, Team Telefund generally receives in cash even more than the total dollars that alumni initially pledged, and expenses for each year's campaign are typically less than 18 cents on the dollar.

A huge digital tote board automatically tracks pledge totals as processing staff enter them from pledge cards retrieved from the student callers. "When the scoreboard is going and we're handing out prizes left and right," said Dowell, "there's no feeling like it."

Yes, prizes. Volunteers receive a free Big Mac from the local McDonald's if they get $100 in donations. For $250, they get a Happy Meal. During one year, enthusiastic callers walked away with more than 600 Happy Meals and 1,300 Big Macs. By Dowell's own tongue-in-cheek calculations, he figures hamburgers inspired donations of more than a quarter of a million dollars.

Other prizes reward the achievement of other annual giving goals as well. When a volunteer receives a gift from a first-time donor, he or she is recognized for Guts and Stamina—G.A.S. for short. A volunteer receiving a first-time gift will yell, "I got G.A.S!" and receive a token good for $2 in gas, of course, at a local station. "I was really excited to get G.A.S.," gushed one student volunteer. "It was a worthwhile challenge to call alumni at the risk of being hung-up on."

And then there is the car. Before 1996, many callers would go home at 8:30 or 9 p.m., leaving calling stations understaffed during the most lucrative hours of the night. Dowell decided to combat the persistent problem of caller attrition by offering a car as a prize. Only callers who remained until the end of a calling session would be eligible for the car drawing at the very end of the campaign. K-State's first major prize to promote caller retention was a 1955 Pontiac Star Chief. Competition was so fierce—and caller retention so strong—that Team Telefund has given a car away every year since.

Students also are first in line to receive other benefits from talking to alumni on the phone. Engineering and veterinary medicine students, for example, find avenues to important internships through contact with alumni. Other callers have received invitations to job interviews. Each night of participation on Team Telefund represents three and a half hours of training for the job skills of selling, marketing, creating networks, and communications.

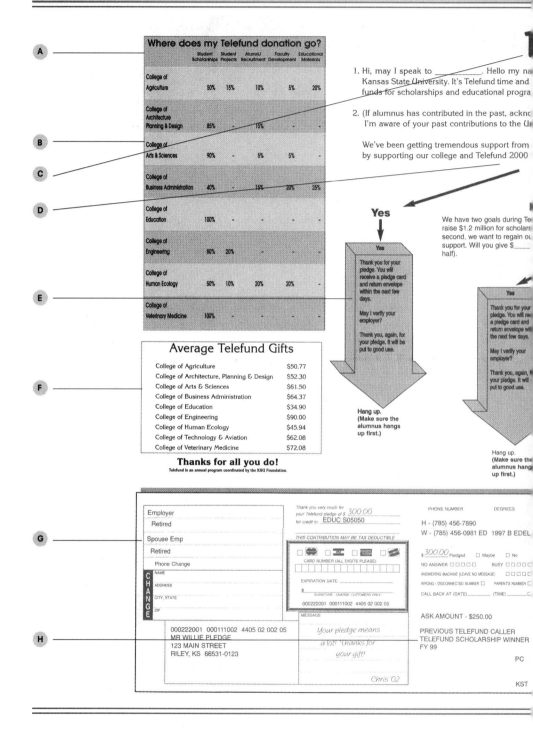

Where does my Telefund donation go?

	Student Scholarships	Student Projects	Alumni/ Recruitment	Faculty Development	Educational Materials
College of Agriculture	50%	15%	10%	5%	20%
College of Architecture Planning & Design	85%	-	15%	-	-
College of Arts & Sciences	90%	-	5%	5%	-
College of Business Administration	40%	-	15%	20%	25%
College of Education	100%	-	-	-	-
College of Engineering	80%	20%	-	-	-
College of Human Ecology	50%	10%	20%	20%	-
College of Veterinary Medicine	100%	-	-	-	-

Average Telefund Gifts

College of Agriculture	$50.77
College of Architecture, Planning & Design	$52.30
College of Arts & Sciences	$61.50
College of Business Administration	$64.37
College of Education	$34.90
College of Engineering	$90.00
College of Human Ecology	$45.94
College of Technology & Aviation	$62.08
College of Veterinary Medicine	$72.08

Thanks for all you do!
Telefund is an annual program coordinated by the KSU Foundation.

1. Hi, may I speak to _____. Hello my na Kansas State University. It's Telefund time and funds for scholarships and educational progra

2. (If alumnus has contributed in the past, ackno I'm aware of your past contributions to the Ur

We've been getting tremendous support from by supporting our college and Telefund 2000

Yes

We have two goals during Te raise $1.2 million for scholars second, we want to regain ou support. Will you give $____ half).

Yes

Thank you for your pledge. You will receive a pledge card and return envelope within the next few days.

May I verify your employer?

Thank you, again, for your pledge. It will be put to good use.

Hang up. (Make sure the alumnus hangs up first.)

Yes

Thank you for your pledge. You will rec a pledge card and return envelope wit the next few days.

May I verify your employer?

Thank you, again, your pledge. It will put to good use.

Hang up. (Make sure the alumnus hang up first.)

Employer
Retired
Spouse Emp
Retired
Phone Change

CHANGE
NAME
ADDRESS
CITY, STATE
ZIP

Thank you very much for your Telefund pledge of $ *300.00*
for credit to EDUC S05050

THIS CONTRIBUTION MAY BE TAX DEDUCTIBLE

CARD NUMBER (ALL DIGITS PLEASE)

EXPIRATION DATE

X
SIGNATURE - CHARGE CUSTOMERS ONLY

000222001 000111002 4405 02 002 05

MESSAGE

000222001 000111002 4405 02 002 05
MR WILLIE PLEDGE
123 MAIN STREET
RILEY, KS 66531-0123

Your pledge means a lot! Thanks for your gift!

Chris '02

PHONE NUMBER   DEGREES

H - (785) 456-7890
W - (785) 456-0981 ED 1997 B EDEL

$ *300.00* Pledged   ☐ Maybe   ☐ No
NO ANSWER ☐☐☐☐   BUSY ☐☐☐☐
ANSWERING MACHINE (LEAVE NO MESSAGE)   ☐☐☐☐
WRONG / DISCONNECTED NUMBER ☐   PARENTS NUMBER ☐
CALL BACK AT (DATE)_____ (TIME)_____ ☐

ASK AMOUNT - $250.00

PREVIOUS TELEFUND CALLER
TELEFUND SCHOLARSHIP WINNER
FY 99

PC

KST

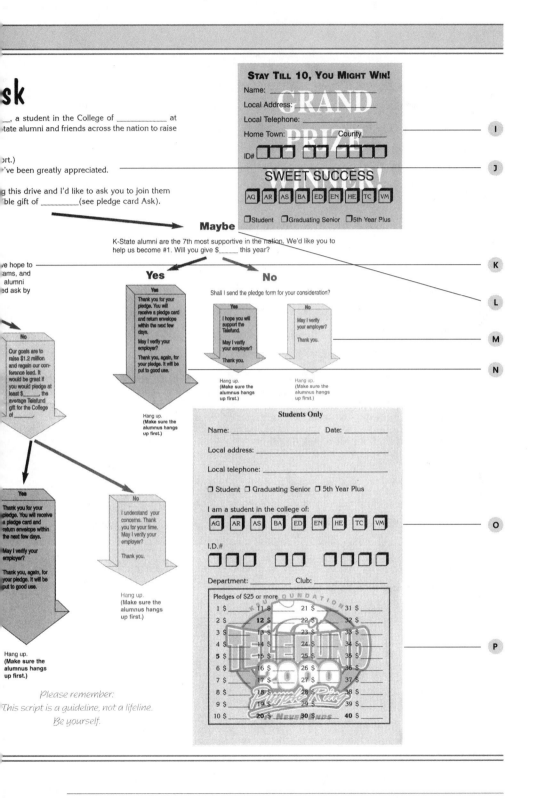

sk

____, a student in the College of _____ at ____
____ tate alumni and friends across the nation to raise

____ ort.)

____ 've been greatly appreciated.

____ g this drive and I'd like to ask you to join them ____
____ ble gift of _____(see pledge card Ask).

STAY TILL 10, YOU MIGHT WIN!

Name: _____

Local Address: _____

Local Telephone: _____

Home Town: _____ County _____

ID# ☐☐☐ ☐☐ ☐☐☐☐

GRAND PRIZE

SWEET SUCCESS!

AG AR AS BA ED EN HE TC VM

☐Student ☐Graduating Senior ☐5th Year Plus

Maybe

K-State alumni are the 7th most supportive in the nation. We'd like you to help us become #1. Will you give $_____ this year?

Yes **No**

Yes
Thank you for your pledge. You will receive a pledge card and return envelope within the next few days.
May I verify your employer?
Thank you, again, for your pledge. It will be put to good use.
Hang up. (Make sure the alumnus hangs up first.)

Shall I send the pledge form for your consideration?

Yes
I hope you will support the Telefund.
May I verify your employer?
Thank you.
Hang up. (Make sure the alumnus hangs up first.)

No
May I verify your employer?
Thank you.
Hang up. (Make sure the alumnus hangs up first.)

No
Our goals are to raise $1.2 million and regain our conference lead. It would be great if you would pledge at least $_____ the average Telefund gift for the College of _____.

Yes
Thank you for your pledge. You will receive a pledge card and return envelope within the next few days.
May I verify your employer?
Thank you, again, for your pledge. It will be put to good use.
Hang up. (Make sure the alumnus hangs up first.)

No
I understand your concerns. Thank you for your time. May I verify your employer?
Thank you.
Hang up. (Make sure the alumnus hangs up first.)

Please remember:
This script is a guideline, not a lifeline.
Be yourself.

Students Only

Name: _____ Date: _____

Local address: _____

Local telephone: _____

☐ Student ☐ Graduating Senior ☐ 5th Year Plus

I am a student in the college of:

AG AR AS BA ED EN HE TC VM

I.D.#

☐☐☐ ☐☐ ☐☐☐☐

Department: _____ Club: _____

Pledges of $25 or more			
1 $ ____	11 $ ____	21 $ ____	31 $ ____
2 $ ____	12 $ ____	22 $ ____	32 $ ____
3 $ ____	13 $ ____	23 $ ____	33 $ ____
4 $ ____	14 $ ____	24 $ ____	34 $ ____
5 $ ____	15 $ ____	25 $ ____	35 $ ____
6 $ ____	16 $ ____	26 $ ____	36 $ ____
7 $ ____	17 $ ____	27 $ ____	37 $ ____
8 $ ____	18 $ ____	28 $ ____	38 $ ____
9 $ ____	19 $ ____	29 $ ____	39 $ ____
10 $ ____	20 $ ____	30 $ ____	40 $ ____

Controlled Chaos: Gordon Dowell uses hundreds of student volunteers in the K-State phonathon each year. To educate them on the basics of a good phone call as quickly as possible, he provides students with a quick reference placemat for use at their calling stations. Here's a guide to what's on it...

A. **The "Brand:"** The Telefund brand is everywhere. It's what alumni recognize, and it helps keep the enthusiasm level high.

B. **Gift Designations:** For alumni who want to know what their gift does, students have at their fingertips gift designations for the eight different units.

C. **Sample Script:** A sample script, "The Ask," provides a guide for the students who are new at calling. Note the continued reinforcement of the Telefund brand.

D. **The Ask Structure:** Dowell has his students ask three times for a gift. Suggested ask amounts are on pledge cards printed for each prospect.

E. **A Pledge!** The finely tuned gift processing staff will put the pledge on the system while calling is still going on, and the pledge will be added to the computerized tote board for the night.

F. **Average Gift Amounts:** By telling students what typical gifts are for each unit, they can work to exceed last year's results and push for donors to increase their giving.

G. **Prospect Pledge Card:** It's designed to occupy this exact space (now *that's* attention to detail). Note the prominent emphasis on credit card gifts in the middle and the special space for students to add a personal note when a pledge is received. The pledge card is sent as a confirmation in the next day's mail.

H. **Alumni Involvements:** Any alumni involvements noted on the alumni database are listed here.

I. **Drawing Registration:** No student is eligible for the car drawing unless they stay until 10 p.m. on the calling night. Lots of other prizes reward students who help to achieve Telefund's many goals.

J. The Bandwagon: K-State's calling scripts are full of references to strong alumni gift support. The K-State Telefund doesn't just ask for a gift, it reinforces a giving culture.

K. One More Try: Before the student caller gives up, he/she references the Big 12 Conference. If the alumnus won't support K-State leading the Big 12 Conference in alumni giving, what will they ever support?

L. Maybe? While not encouraged, students can ask alumni to consider a gift later. The pledge card will be sent to these undecided alumni in the hope that they'll decide to give.

M. Don't Hang Up! Telefund rules require the student to allow the alumnus to hang up first.

N. Verify Employment Information: By always confirming employment information, the university gains greater insight into where its matching gifts might be hiding... not to mention a major donor or two.

O. Tear-Off Student Calling Card: Careful accounting keeps track of every student and what college they are from. This allows for great accumulation of statistics, even in a non-computerized environment.

P. Pledge Tally Card: Students record each pledge they receive over $25. Milestone prizes are earned at each bold gift number. Sure, it's old-fashioned, but the program raises nearly $2 million each year.

A TRADITION OF EXUBERANT GIVING

But volunteers are driven by much more than the chance at winning prizes, upgrading social and professional skills, and making contacts. They are also driven by tradition. "It's all about creating energy," said Dowell. "Whether it's the student callers, the alumni, the faculty, the media, the corporate underwriters, or anyone else within earshot, I want them to get excited about this program."

Since joining the program in 1987, Dowell has been doing just that. During his tenure, Dowell has seen contributions to the annual fund from Team Telefund

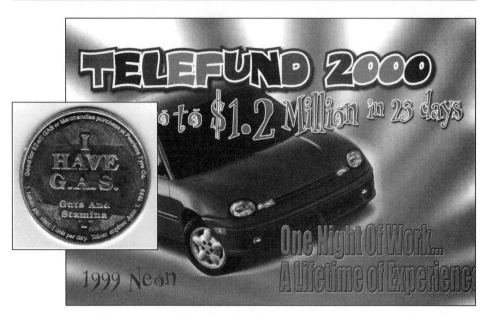

K-State students win tokens good for free gas when they demonstrate "Guts And Stamina" by persuading alumni to make first-time gifts. One student wins a car.

rise from $338,000 in his first year to a goal of $1.8 million in 2003. More important, however, is the fact that students graduate from Kansas State with a deep appreciation of alumni giving. "[Student volunteers are] getting educated about the importance of the Telefund and the importance of giving in support of K-State, and they're buying into a tradition," said Dowell.

For nearly a generation, student callers have reminded alumni of the enthusiastic spirit of volunteerism and school loyalty that Team Telefund inspires. Alumni don't just expect a giving call from K-State; they look forward to it. With more than 30 percent alumni participation, K-State annually ranks at or near the top among its Big 12 Conference peers, and also rates well in national comparisons with other state universities, according to the Council for Aid to Education (CAE).

"I really believe that I can engage students as volunteers because they learn that they will encounter a receptive audience more often than you might find at other schools," said Dowell. "This is where I think the tradition of the program has had a positive impact. If we're going to survive in times of telemarketing saturation by all kinds of salespeople, it's going to be because alumni enjoy it as an event and celebrate it as a tradition."

Another critical component is the deep involvement of faculty and staff. "We call it *Team* Telefund for a reason," said Dowell. "I would not be able to recruit nearly enough students without the staff in each college of the university actively promoting the program." A Telefund administrator at each college is in charge of recruiting "leadership students" who then recruit student "coaches" who in turn recruit teams of student callers. "The colleges participate for a good reason. They see the cost-effective way that funds are raised, and they make it a priority to provide staff assistance," said Dowell.

Dowell describes his program the same way many colleges describe their reunions. "We don't have the personality of an East Coast college that cultivates a strong class structure and reunion giving habit. But I am able to use this program to instill in students a tradition and culture of gift support that will stay with them as alumni. I really believe that the annual calling we do is a ritual that is anticipated by alumni and enjoyed by students."

HOOPLA IN THE DEAD OF WINTER

The management structure that provides the backbone to the program is complemented with excitement that runs throughout the calling month. This could not be more deliberate. "It's important for the Telefund to be viewed as a happening. [This] helps as we're recruiting callers," said Dowell. As the program starts, press releases, e-mail updates (to a list of more than 150 people on campus and off), and other public relations pieces provide progressively more exciting news about the program. "The momentum is important. By the time we get halfway through the calling schedule, the schools that remain are excited about the results from the beginning weeks. It can become very self-fulfilling."

Dowell points out that Telefund works because a number of factors fall neatly into place. "We hold it in February. There's nothing else to do in Manhattan. The corporate sponsorship has become a huge deal, with more than 100 companies donating more than $55,000 worth of goods and services as prize incentives. If not for their generosity, I'm not sure it would be as compelling for the students. Also, we have the right size alumni population, approximately 70,000. If we were larger, the logistics would start to boggle the mind. And lastly, I think there is a spirit of volunteerism here that makes it possible to engage the students in the first place."

Good marketing is the seed of contagious participation. Fortunately, Dowell enjoys a flair for promotion. For the 2000 program he installed a Webcam in the phone room. Now any K-State alumnus who is called can access the camera via the Internet and see the live action while they speak on the phone.

To promote caller recruiting, the prize car is periodically parked in conspicuous places around campus before and during the campaign. Students in charge of caller recruitment are issued shirts recognizable campus wide, inviting interested students to conveniently learn more or apply to become a caller.

Each campaign has a theme. Among them was the Tour de Cats, which played off of the school mascot (the wildcat) and the Tour de France bicycle race. At the end of each calling session, leading callers—like the leading riders in the race—were awarded yellow "Stage Leader" jerseys.

LESSON: FIRST KNOW YOUR INSTITUTION

Dowell cautions that the growth of the K-State program cannot be copied without commitment. "I wouldn't tell anyone that I could go to XYZ University and change things overnight. It takes time to build the kind of network we have now. We have built a tradition where our alumni genuinely look forward to the call, with many of them having participated as callers when they were students. I believe we're grounded because we're not just maximizing revenue for this year, we're developing a giving tradition."

A tradition, unlike the latest technologies and phonathon innovations, can't be borrowed or duplicated. Before implementing the next new thing, an annual giving program should examine its last new thing. Fund programs should be based on a foundation in the school's unique people and traditions.

University of Rochester   **3**

Integrating with the Internet

The Rochester Fund arrived online with a single Web page—and
then persuaded alumni to come along as well

There was a time when soliciting alumni by phone and mailing appeal
letters were new and novel fund-raising ideas. More recently, so were the
Internet and e-mail. But Internet sites for annual giving did not immediately set the world on fire. For many schools, an Internet "presence" meant merely
that—a presence on the school's Web site that made reference to annual giving and
not much more. The first annual giving Web pages typically copied information
straight from annual giving brochures. In so doing, most schools gained no additional capabilities from the Internet. They simply created an online place to read the
annual giving brochure.

The pulse quickened some time later with the onset of online gift-receiving
capabilities. Many schools created Web pages that permitted would-be donors to
pledge or donate immediately with credit cards. (Others, in a fit of paper paradigm stubbornness, allowed donors only to download printable paper pledge
forms that they could mail back to the school.)

Even for the schools with new online giving pages, frustrations continued.
They had opened up a new storefront with their giving page, but donors weren't
beating down the doors. Expectations for online fund-raising windfalls went
unfulfilled. Many trailblazing schools told those considering Web pages that
Internet commotion was overblown.

ROCHESTER AT A GLANCE:

UNIVERSITY OF ROCHESTER Rochester, New York	
Nickname	Yellowjackets
Type of institution	Private doctoral/ research university
Founded	1850
Total enrollment	8,490
Endowment market value	$1.131 billion
Total alumni giving for current operations	$8,478,325
Undergraduate alumni of record	47,050
Graduate alumni of record	31,886
Alumni solicited	69,606
Alumni donors	14,844
Participation (of alumni solicited)	21%
Web site	www.rochester.edu

One reason, of course, was that many would-be donors did not even know the online giving pages existed. (Many of them probably still don't.) Schools were revving the engines on their new Internet vehicles, but they weren't firing on all cylinders.

But there were reasons to stick with it. While many alumni still enjoy receiving calls from alma mater, statistics at many schools were trending steadily downward in the number of alumni they were able to get on the phone. Caller ID, unlisted phone numbers, increased usage of cell phones as primary phone numbers, and people who just never seemed to be home (and were less inclined to answer the phone when they were) all seemed to be conspiring against the good old phonathon.

As for direct mail, its demise had already been predicted for years. Long before the arrival of spam e-mail, there was junk snailmail. Postage rates were continuing to rise, and it was increasingly costly to present an elaborate detailed case for annual gift support using printed materials.

In the end, though, some schools began to solve the Internet riddle. What finally enabled the Internet to help annual giving programs become *better* was

The University of Rochester "college" (undergraduate program) used the occasion of the university's 150th anniversary to re-emphasize its alumni-giving culture. Engaging younger alumni proved to be a challenge.

the integration of the Internet with thoughtful marketing strategies that use direct mail and even telemarketing to introduce prospects to new Web communications, appeals, and services. What makes the Internet useful is what it can do that is impossible (or cost-prohibitive) via other methods of communication. For annual giving programs, the Internet offers opportunities to enhance relationships with donors.

FIRST INTERNET FORAY

In 2000, the University of Rochester's Rochester Fund created an annual giving Web page. As at many schools, the Rochester Fund's Web page was, in fact, one single page that described annual giving the same way as did the Rochester Fund's direct mail brochure. (To create the original page, annual giving staff worked with an advancement office Web designer and followed a template consistent with university style guidelines).

Once online, the Rochester Fund's Web page shared another trait common to other schools' annual giving Web pages: No one visited it. Even though the page permitted visitors to make pledges via e-mail (a kind of *faux* online giving), few people visited the new page, and the e-mailbox for receiving online gifts remained mostly empty.

At about the same time no one was visiting his Web page, Gary Simpson, the director of the Rochester Fund, began to think about marketing and the Internet. Simpson had arrived at the university with private-sector brand management experience. Although unfamiliar with the ways of university fund raising, he knew how to create demand by effectively marketing a product.

"In the wake of the big 2001 stock market run-up and the overinflated expectations for online business, things were crashing and a lot of Internet corporations were going out of business," recalled Simpson. "When I met fellow annual giving peers at other schools, they were joining in with their criticism of the Internet. Everyone had set up these pages, and almost no one had anything to show for it. They were jumping to the conclusion that it was a bad idea.

"And yet, my feeling was that we had virtually set the pages up in the middle of a forest—no one knew they were there," added Simpson. "At Rochester, we hadn't done a very good job of telling anybody what was there and why it was a good thing. We had figured out the technology, but we hadn't figured out the marketing."

ADDITION OF ONLINE GIVING

The online giving page was the next big Internet creation initiated by many colleges and universities around the same time. First, they had used the Internet to simply replicate the information in their printed brochures. Now, online giving offered a resource that phone and mail did not—the ability to receive gifts directly with potentially reduced telemarketing, printing, postage, and gift-processing costs.

But there were additional technological hurdles. The Web site now needed a "secure server" that allowed donors to safely provide credit card information to make their gift over the Internet, and the U of R information technology office was able to provide it. (At that time, and even now, many other schools contracted with secure site vendors.)

In May 2001, the University of Rochester was for the first time officially able to receive online gifts. Reminiscent, though, of the debut of the Rochester Fund's original annual giving Web page, online giving was a dud that raised, by Simpson's estimation, "a pittance."

To draw attention to the site, a postcard informed alumni of the new and easy-to-use online giving capabilities, and the Rochester Fund URL (*www.rochester.edu/alumni/rochfund*) was added to all snailmail appeal letters and billings. As more and more audiences learned about the Web capabilities, Simpson realized he was not confined to directing everyone to the same two Web pages. If he could have two Web pages, why not four? Or eight?

"We were telling Rochester parents to visit that same old original annual giving Web page, and it dawned on me that we could easily create a Parent Fund Web page, one that could be much more interesting and compelling to parents," said Simpson.

From one page came several, each with its own audience and messages, starting with separate branding of the Rochester Fund and the Parent Fund. (In subsequent years, reunions have come to have a prominent place as well.)

A donor's particular circumstances drove ideas for new pages as well. "We were encouraging people to go online and make an immediate credit card gift, we had people who wanted to go online to make a pledge, and we had people who had already made a pledge and wanted to pay it off," said Simpson. "So, you really had a need for three more pages that had options and messages customized for three different sets of circumstances."

IF YOU BUILD IT, WILL THEY COME?

Simpson's marketing advanced another step the following annual giving year. The Rochester Fund had wrestled with the problem of low young-alumni-giving participation, with the university's youngest alumni decreasingly responding to

Step #1

The university mails young alumni a CD-ROM that features downloadable screensavers and a paper pledge card—for alumni who want to contribute the old-fashioned way.

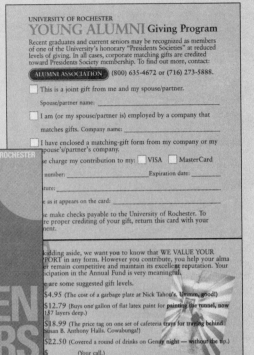

Step #2

The screensaver program introduces alumni to online giving and Rochester's new online alumni community.

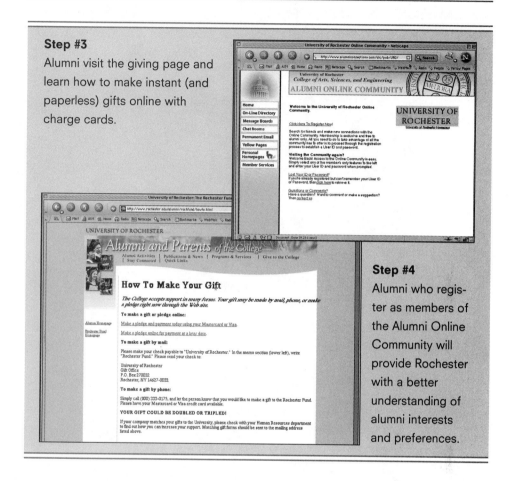

Step #3

Alumni visit the giving page and learn how to make instant (and paperless) gifts online with charge cards.

Step #4

Alumni who register as members of the Alumni Online Community will provide Rochester with a better understanding of alumni interests and preferences.

traditional direct mail appeals (See Chapter 5, "Reed College: The Lesson of Lemmings"). Why wasn't the Rochester Fund message connecting with younger alumni? In addition to the message, could the problem also be the old-fashioned paper-mail *medium* that was delivering the message?

Over in the Rochester alumni office, the same questions were being asked. The alumni relations office was exploring plans for a first-ever online "alumni community." This new alumni relations Internet site would provide an online alumni directory, class notes, up-to-date campus news, and other resources that would sustain alumni affinity and involvement with the university. Their concerns were similar: How do we motivate alumni to come to the site and learn about the resources that are there?

Step #1

The university sends all alumni a "pre-call" postcard alerting them that the Rochester Fund phonathon will be beginning in the next few days and that they can expect a call from a student...

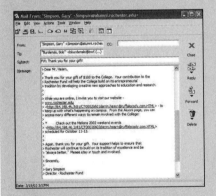

Step #2

As callers receive pledges over the phone, they ask alumni to provide e-mail addresses at which they can receive e-mail confirmations of their pledges.

Step #3

E-mail confirmations sent the next day confirm the gift and refer alumni to the online giving Web site.

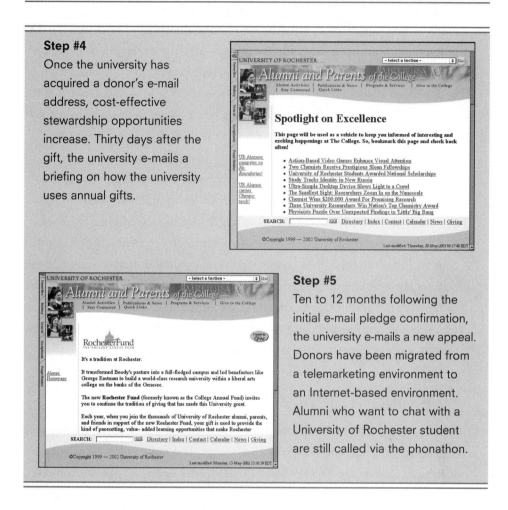

Step #4

Once the university has acquired a donor's e-mail address, cost-effective stewardship opportunities increase. Thirty days after the gift, the university e-mails a briefing on how the university uses annual gifts.

Step #5

Ten to 12 months following the initial e-mail pledge confirmation, the university e-mails a new appeal. Donors have been migrated from a telemarketing environment to an Internet-based environment. Alumni who want to chat with a University of Rochester student are still called via the phonathon.

It was obvious to Simpson and other staff members that younger alumni were increasingly likely to use e-mail as their primary means of communication. To reach them, the university first needed to get those alumni e-mail addresses.

Postcards were suggested as a tool to introduce young alumni to the Web content, but Simpson wanted to do more. "How could we give them something they would want? How can we get their attention?"

At that time, companies like America Online were mailing prospects CD-ROMs to market their subscription service. It was a clever use of an existing communications method (snailmail) to promote a new communications method (the online world).

Simpson told the advancement division's publications staff what he was thinking, and they came up with the idea for screensavers—a high-tech gift that linked alumni's good feelings for the university to their computers. (In today's era of increasing high-speed Internet access, such screensavers are more likely to be downloaded direct from a university's Web site. As Simpson contemplated the idea in 2001, when download speeds were a much bigger concern, he feared that alumni would get impatient and give up.) In the end, the staff thought the CD-ROM would intrigue people enough to put it in and see what it was.

Once loaded onto a computer, the screensaver automatically ran through a multimedia commercial message on behalf of the Rochester Fund. When completed, a menu of options offered viewers the ability to load the screensavers and more.

The screensaver CD-ROM became a gateway to all sorts of new U of R Internet content, including the annual giving pages, a new online alumni community, and a personal profile alumni could edit online. "The CD served an important purpose of showing our young alumni that we could communicate with them in a high-tech way and introducing them to a lot of value-added content on our Web site that we thought they would enjoy," said Simpson.

FINISHING TOUCHES

The final piece of track in the marketing railroad was set in 2002. Alumni were increasingly utilizing the university's Web pages, and in FY 2002 online gifts had increased substantially. The Rochester Fund was still operating passively, however, in its efforts to migrate to new methods of communications with the university. Could they be more assertive?

Although the U of R had been requesting alumni e-mail addresses for more than a year, many were still missing and little had been done with the ones already collected. To boost the number, the university's telemarketing vendor offered an intriguing suggestion: Offer every alumnus that made a Rochester Fund pledge by phone an opportunity to receive e-mail confirmation of their gift. (In 2001, the IRS cooperated by agreeing to accept e-mail receipts as evidence of charitable donations.) Simpson improved upon the idea by suggesting that the confirmations include a link so recipients could make gifts online. Ultimately the messages, like the original CD–ROM, exposed alumni to all kinds of Rochester links: Web giving, alumni community, and their online alumni profile.

As with the creation of online giving pages, Simpson was able to create different pages addressed to different donors—donors who had made phonathon pledges, donors who had pledged and paid, and donors who had said "maybe."

Now that the university was communicating with donors online, they started communicating more proactively. "Like a lot of alumni at other schools, the perception of our alumni is that they hear from us only when we're asking them for money," said Simpson. "Well, with all of these new e-mail addresses from our donors, we had a perfect opportunity to communicate information in a way that wasn't a solicitation."

The Rochester Fund now sends e-mail messages that provide donors with periodic updates on how their gifts are being used. The kind of stewardship that used to be cost-prohibitive is now easily and inexpensively available via e-mail.

Simpson's next plans will involve an online solicitation, and the potential for even more significant growth of the university's online relationship with its alumni donors. "Their second-most-frequent complaint is that we interrupt dinner with our phone calls. So, what if we e-mailed them in advance and offered them an alternative?"

Now there's value-added Internet content.

ATTACK OF THE KILLER APPS

The Internet is increasingly valuable to annual giving programs as a tool for sustaining alumni affinity and strengthening relationships with donors. When it speeds processes, it can save money, too. These Internet "killer applications" transcend pre-existing phone and paper communications and make the Web a powerful resource. Here are some of my favorites "killer apps":

- **Duke University** transmits a monthly e-mail newsletter that gives donors an accounting of how the university is using their gifts. Previous newsletters are archived on the Duke Web site. (*www.duke.edu*)

- **The University of Durham** in the U.K. posts profiles and photographs of students who participate in its phonathon program each semester. Alumni can read first-person quotes from the callers describing their post-graduate plans and feelings of pride toward the university. (*www.dur.ac.uk*)

- **Kansas State University** provides a live Webcam view of its student phonathon room (all 75 callers strong). Alumni can get a visual idea of the on-campus program's energy and enthusiasm. (*www.ksu.edu*)

- **North Carolina State University's** annual giving Web site features a video appeal from an NCSU student challenging alumni to "answer the call" by making a pledge to the NC State Annual Fund. (*www.ncsu.edu*)

- **Princeton University's** class Web pages, managed by volunteer members of each class, integrate information about class notes, reunions, photos from past events, and class annual giving goals and results. (*www.princeton.edu*)

- **St. Lawrence University** provides a weekly update of progress toward its annual giving fund-raising goal. The site also lists 10+ years worth of class fund-raising records. (*web.stlawu.edu*)

- **Sweet Briar College** accepts installment credit card pledges via its simple and secure online giving site. The college finds that, over the course of a year, donors who make small recurring payments are more likely to contribute larger total sums than single-payment donors. (*www.sbc.edu*)

- **UCLA** provides its Chancellor's Associates (leadership annual donors) with an online schedule of member events, as well as the opportunities to RSVP directly and immediately via the UCLA Fund Web site. (*www.ucla.edu*)

They Created A Better Culture

Educating Students About Giving

When the university sought to increase alumni gift support,
the lessons started with Stanford students

When schools speak of their "alumni-giving culture," it's usually either in celebration or frustration. Either the school has enjoyed strong alumni-giving support for generations, or it expects that it never will. It's hard to find an institution that is planting the seeds of a giving culture because the returns on these efforts—especially with younger prospects—can be low initially. Consequently, many schools make the attempt, but few stick with it.

Stanford University is one of those few. While alumni have long been proud of their Stanford education, a strong alumni-giving culture has developed only over the past 10 years. While lots of effort from many staff and programs has contributed to Stanford's remarkable alumni-giving growth, emphasis on student development has played a contributing role and set the stage for alumni-giving growth to come.

The phrase "student development," when it has any fund-raising meaning at a university at all, typically refers to a senior gift campaign—an annual giving appeal targeting graduating seniors offered as a crash course on gift support. In fact, it often does crash. Senior gift programs are often much less education than solicitation, with poor timing, poor planning, and poor graduating students reducing them to afterthoughts for both seniors and development staff.

The student development program at Stanford University is not new. Way back in 1994, then-President Gerhard Casper announced that, as a personal priority, he would increase the pool of unrestricted financial resources available for

STANFORD AT A GLANCE:

STANFORD UNIVERSITY Palo Alto, California	
Nickname	The Cardinal
Type of institution	Private doctoral/ research university
Founded	1891
Total enrollment	16,561
Endowment market value	$7.61 billion
Total alumni giving for current operations	$64,360,318
Undergraduate alumni of record	78,464
Graduate alumni of record	71,694
Alumni solicited	148,570
Alumni donors	45,243
Participation (of alumni solicited)	30%
Web site	www.stanford.edu

undergraduate education projects on campus. His declaration set in motion a number of initiatives that placed new emphasis on annual giving and promoted broad new alumni-giving participation in the Stanford Fund, the university's campus-wide annual giving program.

The resulting fund-raising changes included creation of a new reunion-based annual giving structure, a structure used by many private universities but not previously embraced by Stanford. This new fund-raising structure, in turn, placed increased emphasis on class giving and the need to develop a class-giving culture among current students. Before President Casper's announcement, student participation in the previous year's senior gift program had been a dismal 8 percent. Casper pledged to inspire Stanford students to play stronger supporting roles in their university.

A GIVING CULTURE CURRICULUM

Casper backed his pledge with personal involvement—something the students noticed. It became routine for the president to meet with the student committees that headed up the senior gift drive. "It was obvious to all of the seniors that it was important to the president, and I can't tell you how important that was to the program," said Suzanne Mendoza, director of Stanford's student development program. "It's such a powerful reinforcement when students can see the program is a priority of the institution's leadership. Being involved as a student volunteer almost became a status thing. His personal involvement provided credibility, and I think it was critical to the growth of the program."

For several years the university considered ways to instill in students a giving culture that would endure after they became alumni. This awareness building began with a basic explanation of the mission and goals of the Stanford Fund itself. "The emphasis on funding for undergraduate education was a case that was easy to make to the students. They understood the opportunities, even if they weren't going to be around to enjoy all the benefits. The Stanford Fund was about supporting initiatives that benefited their own undergraduate education, as well as that of students to come," said Mendoza.

Stanford creatively identified opportunities for linking in students' minds messages of alumni community and affinity, philanthropy, and the Stanford Fund. Over time, an evolving progression of sponsored events and marketing opportunities provided students with opportunities to learn about the Stanford Fund and the university's alumni-giving culture each year of their four-year undergraduate experience. These opportunities include:

Freshman Thank-a-Thon

The Freshman Thank-a-Thon is an annual weeklong event each fall during which new freshmen voluntarily call alumni to thank them for their gifts over the past year. While other annual giving programs might use paid student telemarketing callers for thank-you calling (if they do it at all), the Stanford Fund capitalizes on the opportunity to personally thank contributors at the same time it educates its newest students about the university's philanthropic traditions. Upwards of 500 students annually volunteer to participate.

The Thank-a-Thon is promoted through class leadership structures (officers, hall representatives, etc.). By recruiting and organizing classmates this way, the program reinforces class identity among the still-new students. Many students participate in order to meet new classmates; it's one of the few volunteer opportunities on campus that is organized on the basis of class and that facilitates interaction among classmates.

Sophomore Academic Dinners

The Stanford Fund and the sophomore class officers host a series of three dinners at which sophomores who have not yet declared majors receive opportunities to speak with alumni and faculty about possible fields of study. During the dinners, an alumni speaker makes a brief announcement to promote the Stanford Fund and introduce students to the university's community of alumni, students, and staff.

Gatherings where students begin to see that alumni care about their success are opportune occasions for connecting themes of alumni loyalty and gift support. "We help underwrite the cost of the event, and we gain an opportunity to educate students further about the Stanford Fund while showing them the ongoing sense of affinity felt by our alumni," said Mendoza.

Junior Networking Night

The Stanford Fund, in conjunction with the career services and alumni relations offices, sponsors a forum for juniors to discuss internship opportunities with alumni employers. Similar to the sophomore academic dinners, Junior Networking Night gives students access to real-world alumni networking situations. The event builds additional name recognition for the Stanford Fund and re-emphasizes the strong affinity and sense of responsibility many alumni feel for the university.

Stanford Student Calling Program

Like many campuses, Stanford conducts its own yearly on-campus phonathon, with paid Stanford students manning the phones. Although the program does not involve a large number of students, it's an additional opportunity for students to learn the reasons for giving and to see first-hand the many alumni that support the university each year. In many years, student callers serve a volunteer role with the Senior Gift campaign.

The Stanford Student Calling Program diverges from the other student development initiatives in one important respect: It is selective about who participates. Because asking for a gift is more difficult than writing thank-you letters or placing thank-you phone calls, the Student Calling Program follows rigorous training and caller-evaluation guidelines.

Stanford Fund Student Group Partnership

The Stanford Fund Student Group Partnership program invites on-campus student groups to write thank-you letters to donors. The idea originated, in part, as an effort to curtail the student groups' annual efforts to solicit alumni directly for support of their activities. The development office budgeted funds to compensate student groups for their thank-you-letter-writing work. The student groups, in return, earned funds for their student group activities.

The program educates a broad student population about alumni philanthropy while providing additional stewardship for Stanford Fund alumni contributors. The program has produced in excess of 18,000 letters annually.

Senior Class Gift

The Senior Class Gift program is an annual fund-raising campaign at many colleges and universities. At Stanford, the class gift is the first class-based effort to solicit gifts for the Stanford Fund. The program assumed additional importance because of the university's new longer-term emphasis on reunion-giving growth.

The Stanford Senior Class Gift campaign begins each fall with the gathering of a committee of students who lead the drive and lend their names to appeal letters and class-cultivation get-togethers. To reinforce feelings of community, alumni as well as the Parents' Advisory Board provide challenge grants. Challenge funds used to match gifts made by graduating seniors serve as an extra motivation for giving.

It's noteworthy that the student co-chairpersons of the Senior Class Gift campaign can reference the Stanford Fund in their appeals—confident that classmates already know what they're talking about. Because of the previous four years' marketing and awareness building, the Senior Class Gift program immediately benefits from a better-educated student prospect audience.

STANFORD STUDENTS RESPOND

The students responded. During the year the president announced the new unrestricted giving priority and demonstrated his willingness to personally advocate

Freshman Thank-a-Thon

Freshmen are recruited to volunteer to call Stanford alumni and thank them for their support. This is the first time many students become aware of Stanford's many alumni donors.

Sophomore Academic Dinners

Sophomores hear alumni speakers talk about their careers. A keynote alumni speaker talks about the Stanford alumni community, the Stanford Fund, and the importance of alumni support to the university and its students.

Junior Networking Night

A forum for juniors to meet with alumni employers and discuss internship opportunities, sponsored by the Stanford Fund.

Student Calling Program

Any Stanford student can work for the on-campus phonathon asking alumni, parents, and friends for annual gifts to the Stanford Fund.

Student Group Partnership

Student groups were prohibited from approaching alumni for gifts, but they could raise funds by writing thank-you letters to Stanford alumni. Over 18,000 a year were written.

Senior Class Gift

Because of the president's personal advocacy on behalf of student giving, the senior gift program grew from 8 percent participation in FY 93 to 78 percent participation in FY 90.

Alumni Culture Dividend?

Alumni-giving percentage at Stanford grew from 22 percent in 1993 to 36 percent in 2000, while senior gift campaign participation grew from 8 percent to 78 percent. Can some of this growth be attributed to proactively teaching students about alumni support and the Stanford Fund?

on behalf of the program to students, the Senior Class Gift program increased participation from 8 percent to a remarkable 44 percent. From 1994 through 2000, student participation in Stanford's Senior Gift campaign increased from 8 percent to a whopping 78 percent. And older Stanford alumni, not to be outdone by the young whippersnappers, increased their giving participation rate by 50 percent over the same period (see page 62).

Casper announced his retirement from Stanford in spring, 2000, and in one of his final speeches as president specifically cited the growth of the Senior Gift campaign as one of his proudest accomplishments.

Lots of money is spent each year on mailings, phone calls, and reunions in an effort to teach alumni about the importance of their gift support. As the Stanfords, Princetons, Wellesleys, and other schools have demonstrated, it can be much more effective to teach these lessons to alumni—before they are alumni.

WELLESLEY COLLEGE:
A POST-GRADUATION SENIOR GIFT PROGRAM

Wellesley College runs a highly effective senior giving program, with participation annually in excess of 80 percent. Wellesley's problem: what to do the year following all the senior class giving hoopla.

The answer came from a trustee who came up with a good idea and a matching gift challenge. The trustee issued the challenge specifically to now-graduated young alumnae class members who had made a gift to the previous year's senior appeal program. She would personally match any gift made by new alumnae during the year after their graduation.

The trustee's challenge effectively let the new class know that their giving was important to the college at any level, and it reminded them of the college's philanthropic culture and tradition of alumnae gift support. As a final culture-reinforcing touch, members of the class who contributed to the trustee's challenge were listed in a special giving society: The Nancy Circle, named after the trustee herself.

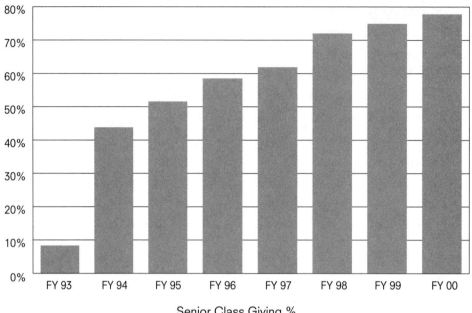

Senior Class Giving %

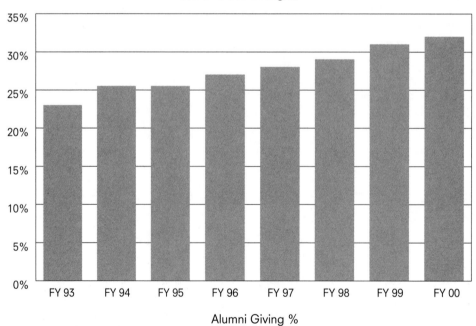

Alumni Giving %

At Stanford, senior-class-giving participation growth paralleled an alumni-giving participation rate that increased steadily for 10 years.

Source: Stanford University, Council for Aid to Education

The Lesson of Lemmings

Reed College connected with young alumni by inventing
a giving society that is uniquely its own

Lemmings are popularly known for spectacular migrations that end up with their crowding into the sea or tumbling off cliffs. Several years ago, a campus publication had likened lemmings to graduating Reed College students tumbling into the real world. This analogy also illustrates how colleges have a hard time building and maintaining alumni-giving relationships with recent graduates. As graduates go forth, awash in the sea of professional life, they can quickly become disconnected from the alma mater—especially if graduates did not receive opportunities to view the role of alumni giving while on campus.

At many institutions, the senior gift program near the end of a student's college career represents the first serious alumni contact. But at Reed College, where the atmosphere is different from many institutions of higher learning, a senior gift program is not a good fit. Deep dedication not just to academics but also to the academic life is palpable on campus. The academic program intensifies through senior year, making gift coordination excessively difficult. Also, senior gift programs generate attention but not a great deal of student discourse. Because discourse is a fundamental aspect of Reed, a senior gift did not engage the spirit on campus.

"When I got to Reed, the complaint was there wasn't any senior class gift program. But I wasn't particularly interested in any senior class gift program," said

REED AT A GLANCE:

REED COLLEGE Portland, Oregon	
Nickname	Reedies
Type of institution	Private liberal arts college
Founded	1908
Total enrollment	1,363
Endowment market value	$325 million
Web site	www.reed.edu

Julie Feely, who served as Reed's director of annual giving from 1992 to 1999 before becoming a major gifts officer at the college. "I've worked on them before, and my thought was that at Reed they wouldn't work. [At Reed,] seniors have to write and defend a thesis in the spring of their senior year. It's a very stressful time, and they're a weary group. Seniors at other schools might be winding down and taking it easy; that's not the case at Reed. [A gift program may be] good at other schools, but it's just not going to happen here."

A HERD OF NON-CONFORMISTS

Deciding that a gift program would not work for Reed was only the first step toward finding a program that *would* work. Something had to be done to cultivate a relationship with students.

To further complicate matters, the alumni association continued to congratulate recent graduates on becoming alumni without making a solicitation. "That was a concern of mine," said Feely. "Well, wait a minute now. We're not doing a senior class gift, and then we send a student a letter that says we're proud that he or she is a member of the alumni association but we're not going to be asking them for money." The message of giving was not clearly coming through.

Feely and her assistant director considered ideas for a more "Reed-like" young alumni-giving program that did not intrude on the senior spring thesis. Too many ideas centered on class giving but, because of the Reed culture and its fluid coursework structure, there isn't a great amount of class identity at Reed.

The irreverent image of the lemming fit the postgraduate mood and provided a Generation X theme that young Reed alumni identified with.

Taking the PLUNGE

You're somewhere between here and there. Well on your way toward becoming a distinguished Reed alum. You spent four (or five, or six, or seven) years marching toward that towering precipice, a place where college ends. You ran forward, sometimes losing your footing on the fleeting ground of college life. You turned and briefly glanced back at us one last time . . . . Then, like a certain species of furry-footed rodent, you took one more step . . . and plunged into the Real World.

Now, plummeting through the air, struggling to accustom yourself to the unforeseen chaos of reality, you probably aren't overly concerned with "giving something back" to Reed. Yet we are unwilling to let the specter of certain failure deter us from our duties, and we decided to get clever. (Never has the old adage, "there's a fine line between clever and stupid," been more true.) Think of it this way: we aren't really asking you for money. What we have instead is an offer: a chance to be a member of a distinguished gift society.

But aren't members of gift societies normally austere, upright, filthy rich individuals who are pillars of their communities?

Well, yes, until now. It just didn't seem fair that gift societies cost so much for such recent graduates. So we've started the **Reed College Lemming Society**—just for young alumni (Classes of '87–'95) who give $10 (or more) to Reed. For all your trouble and sacrifice, you will receive your very own, pocket-sized Reed College Lemming Society membership card!

And for the lucky lemmings who join by June 28, 1996, you get an added bonus. Your contribution will be tripled in value via the Chairman's Challenge, a generous grant made by Walter Mintz '50, trustee and chair of the Campaign for Reed College. This is how it works:

- All NEW gifts of $10 or more will be matched two-for-one. (New gifts are defined as those given by donors who did not give last year.)

- All INCREASES of gifts over the previous year will be matched two-for-one.

—Written in collaboration with Ethan Ladd '94 and Rachel Hall '95

Surprisingly, their brainstorming eventually led to a small furry animal. Years before, the endearing article about lemmings had achieved some notoriety on campus. Feely and her staff wondered if lemmings could possibly serve as an image for promoting philanthropy.

THE LINE BETWEEN CLEVER AND STUPID

The Lemming Society was created to motivate young alumni to give. The theme blended the image of recent graduates hurled into the real world with a lampoon of the stereotype of stuffy "grown-up" giving societies.

At first, Feely's staff balked. "We said, 'We can't do the lemming thing.' The implications of animals jumping off cliffs together troubled us," said Feely. Nevertheless, the concept had appeal. "The idea was created by a Reedie (Reed alumnus) and it was created in fun."

Initial discussions with the alumni office generated more trepidation. "You have to be careful with humor," said Feely, "because humor can really explode on you." The annual giving staff knew they were pushing the envelope, and they were careful to think through the rationale for their idea. They were very aware that if the humor did in fact explode, alumni complaints would be directed at the president and the appeal chair.

Mustering up their courage, the staff presented the alumni office with a proposal for increasing young alumni giving that directly identified the problem of low involvement. They offered solutions that proposed less formalized communication strategies appropriate for reaching younger donors. By emphasizing the larger strategy of alumni communication and by presenting objectives and methods that would achieve the program's goals, Feely and her staff got the Lemming Society idea considered fairly on its merits.

Feedback on the proposed program from graduating Reed students was overwhelmingly positive. "They loved the idea. So, we asked two students to write the initial letters and brochure text themselves," said Feely. "What they wrote was hilarious. I know I couldn't have done it myself. They have the experience and background to say things in a context to their peers that I don't have."

One tagline read "Reed College Lemming Society: A Club That's Not." Another encouraged the recent graduates to "Take the Plunge" by making their lemming-like gift. A pocket-sized Lemming Society membership card entitled

YOUR NEXT CHANCE
TO BECOME A LEMMING...

• Soon, a current Reedie will call and ask you to join the Lemming Society if you're a Reed alumni in the classes of 1988-96.

• Say yes, and pledge at $10 or more to the 1996-97 Annual Fund.

• When your 1996-97 Reed College [...] Society membership card comes in the [...] will be official! You're a Lemming.

REED COLLEGE LEMMING SOCI[...]
A Club That's Not

P.S. Ask the caller to tell you about how [...] is matched two-for-one by the Ch[...] Challenge.

The Reed College Lemming Society

Reed college promoted the Lemming Society as "A Club That's Not" with a membership card that provided "no benefits whatsoever."

donors to "run among lemmings" and proudly offered absolutely no other benefits. The tongue-in-cheek appeal observed that, "Never has the old adage, 'There's a fine line between clever and stupid' been more true."

The message deliberately contrasted the new society with older giving societies and traditional recognition listings. Longstanding alumni and friends of Reed College may be attracted to the honor and tradition of giving groups like the Amanda Reed Society ($10,000+), the Griffin Society ($1,000-$5,000), or the Eliot Circle ($500+). The Lemming Society targeted students and young alumni (those who had graduated within the last nine years) who not only value fun and humor, but who are also likely to be more concerned with adjusting to a starting salary than contributing significantly to an annual fund.

"We are lucky to be in an environment where people are able to take some risks," Feely said. "At Reed, the idea is, 'If you can find a solution to the problem, give it a try. We're going to let you go with it.'" The plan obtained the approval of the annual fund chair, the vice president, and the president. Several mailings and a phonathon effort comprised the first Lemming Society appeal. They braced for the worst.

Leadership's concerns quickly proved unfounded. Recent graduates began to give, in stampedes. "Our president began to tell everyone about it everywhere he went. He liked the way it was quirky and emblematic of a college that, in a distinguishing way, was quirky as well," said Feely.

RESULTS OF CALCULATED RISK

A priority for the program was involvement — getting young alumni to make *any* gift to the annual giving program and thus establishing a giving habit that would produce larger gifts over time. For that purpose, the Lemming Society appeal recognized any gift above $10. Gifts were also matched two-for-one through funds pledged by the annual fund chair (yes, the Lemming Chairman's Challenge), effectively tripling the program's revenue. In FY 1995, before the program's inception, the annual giving program had 266 young alumni donors. By the end of FY 1996, they had 381 young Lemming donors, a participation increase of almost 40 percent. Participation rates continued to grow, and by FY 1999 the Lemming Society had 550 members, a 72 percent increase from 1995. Feely credited the young alumni program for contributing to an overall doubling of annual giving income over the same time period.

The program's continued growth inspired new marketing initiatives for current students and may even lead to the creation of the senior gift program Feely initially sought to avoid. The Lemming Society brand has become a campus rallying point that Feely has leveraged into other student- and recent-graduate-giving opportunities. "The lemming image has been so useful with the younger

The Chairman's Challenge

And you thought that the most important contribution you made to Reed was your senior thesis. . . .

CHAIRMAN'S CHALLENGE TRIPLES GIFTS

Thanks to Walter Mintz '50, trustee and chair of the Campaign for Reed College, alumni in reunion years and young alumni can triple their gifts to Reed this year through the Chairman's Challenge. The challenge was established by Mintz to encourage new and increased Annual Fund gifts from these two special alumni groups.

Reunion years provide an opportunity for alumni to consider what Reed has meant in their lives, return to campus, and celebrate with old friends and new. It is also a time when many alumni make special gifts in honor of their Reed education. The Chairman's Challenge offers an added incentive by matching two for one all new gifts, or any increase in a previous year's gift, from alumni in the classes of 1947, 1957, 1967, 1972, 1977, and 1987.

For recent graduates, those in the classes of 1988–96, all new and increased gifts will also be matched two for one by the Chairman's Challenge. These alumni are also eligible to join the newly re-established Lemming Society. The Lemming Society, a gift club for recent graduates who give $10 or more, was revived this past spring and was met with great enthusiasm from the more than 350 young alumni who participated.

The Annual Fund is a signficant part of the Campaign for Reed College, contributing $10 million of the $80 million goal. Gifts to the Annual Fund are a critical source of unrestricted revenue for Reed and go directly to where the needs are greatest, including student financial aid, faculty salaries, library and computer acquisitions, and more. Last year more than 5,000 donors contributed more than $1,750,000 to the Annual Fund, the most successful year to date.

The Lemming Society captured the fancy of the college's campaign chairman, who announced that he would triple the value of Lemming Society gifts from young Reedies.

audience that we've started to get the name and the images out through sponsorship of various student events. By the time they graduate, our students have been exposed to the Lemming Society and know what it's all about."

LESSON OF THE LEMMINGS

The success of the Lemming Society has given Feely new insights. "I've come to think of our prospects as moving targets now. The Lemming Society has been a great hook for the young-alumni population, but we're now thinking about how to further build their loyalty beyond the initial fashion we created with the lemming idea. They're still not ready to embrace some of the conventional appeals and giving societies. We're looking for the next new thing."

Feely's advice to other institutions: "If you're going to go out on a limb with something, you have to make sure it's within the context of that institution's mission. Reed is an institution that thrives on individual intellectual pursuits. The concept and promotion of the Lemming Society was emblematic of the institution."

Annual giving programs sometimes suffer from a pack mentality; they use the same gift programs, giving levels, appeal letters, and strategies as their peers. This is not always to an institution's disadvantage. Proven methods should be shared and replicated, but each institution should recognize the unique qualities of its student body and alumni and, when appropriate, consider breaking away into new territory. Even if it means becoming a lemming.

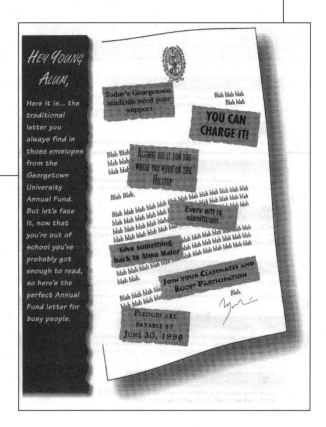

The Blah Blah Blah Letter has been sent to young alumni by numerous schools over the years.

The Same Old Blah Blah Blah

The Lemming Society owes its pedigree, in part, to the ubiquitous "blah blah blah" young-alumni appeal letter that has been bouncing around for nearly 10 years. The origin of the letter is cloudy, but it's known to have existed as early as 1996 (Georgetown University) and as recently as 2002 (Grand Valley State University).

One of the first attempts to make fun of annual giving appeals, the letter superimposes key message points over (literally) lines of "blah blah" text. It was a hit with young alumni, who understood that the letter was obviously directed to them and that the university was aware that they could not afford the same gifts as wealthier older alumni.

Managing Volunteers for Success

A CASE Circle of Excellence Award recipient found that achieving
fund-raising goals still begins with effective volunteers

P hillips Exeter Academy is among a handful of independent schools whose history spans more than 200 years. Its annual giving program, by comparison, is a relatively recent arrival, dating back only to 1922. Since its beginning, the Exeter Annual Giving Fund has grown mightily, and in FY 2002 Exeter became the first secondary school to raise $5 million in annual gifts in a single year. The New Hampshire school's fund-raising prowess has made it a regular recipient of the CASE Circle of Excellence Award for overall fund-raising performance. With more than 50 percent of the academy's 17,000 alumni—known as "Exonians"—giving annually, graduates play an important role in sustaining the school's record-setting fund-raising pace.

Central to a Phillips Exeter Academy education is the Harkness table (see page 75), the omnipresent place where students learn to actively participate in discussions. Not surprisingly, participating students become participating donors after graduation.

According to Wayne Loosigian, director of annual giving, the outstanding rate of alumni giving results from the dedication and hard work of more than 300 volunteers who each year donate their time in support of the annual giving program. The school's historical reputation for excellence, combined with an annual giving program that has carefully and deliberately established a culture of volunteer commitment, produces volunteers who often ask to be involved and devote significant amounts of time helping the program reach its fund-raising goals.

PHILLIPS EXETER AT A GLANCE:

PHILLIPS EXETER ACADEMY Exeter, New Hampshire	
Nickname	Big Red
Type of institution	Private preparatory school
Founded	1781
Total enrollment	1,007
Endowment market value	$520 million
Total alumni giving for current operations	$4,622,483
Undergraduate alumni of record	20,293
Graduate alumni of record	81,146
Alumni solicited	16,789
Alumni donors	8,650
Participation (of alumni solicited)	52%
Web site	www.exeter.edu

The well-oiled volunteer machine was not always so efficient. Improving volunteer performance at Exeter took time, and it evolved in stages. A couple of pivotal events over the years yielded today's Exonian volunteers.

In his early days at the academy, Loosigian was frustrated because volunteers did not effectively fulfill their roles or contribute to the program's success. "We were so busy feeling grateful for their involvement that their involvement alone became the focus and our goal, and the volunteers knew it. They were doing us a favor by being involved, but the important fund-raising work was not getting done. Gifts were not being solicited, and annual giving dollars were not being raised."

Realizing volunteers had little control over the problem, Loosigian decided on his own to change things. "I don't believe fund raising is a democratic process."

EQUAL PARTS AFFECTION AND ACCOUNTABILITY

Although many institutions might balk before demanding greater accountability from volunteers, Loosigian saw both a need and an opportunity to change things. "The academy has always stood for excellence, and I knew our volunteers felt

The Harkness table isn't complete without your **participation**

We're halfway there!

31.1%

Participation makes the Harkness table work.

Thanks to strong and growing support, we are halfway to our goal of 60 percent alumni/ae participation in the 1999-00 Annual Giving Fund. This means we are halfway to completing the annual financial commitment that students and teachers rely on to make the Harkness table work.

Your financial participation in Exeter today is just as critical as your participation around the Harkness table as a student. Please join the growing number

of alumnae and alumni who support the Fund by sending your gift today. Your gift may be of any amount; it's your participation that Exeter values most.

ANNUAL GIVING FUND
PHILLIPS EXETER ACADEMY
phone: (603) 777-3473
fax: (603) 777-4395
email: annualgiving@exeter.edu

What happens at the table...

still depends on *your* participation

Phillips Exeter reminds alumni of its unique Harkness table, a student experience that helps to sustain a culture of alumni annual giving participation.

pride in their continuing involvement. I thought the academy had the right and the ability to expect a higher standard."

Loosigian's mantra became, "When you think of Exeter, think of business." He described the annual giving program to potential volunteers as a business venture of Exeter Academy, and he made it his business to set expectations and ground rules in an upfront, businesslike way. "They know that the program will be run in a first-class manner, and we go out of our way to recognize success and hard work."

Along with all this volunteer accountability, Exeter adds a liberal dose of affection. Loosigian knew, after all, that at the end of the day the volunteers in his business are, well, volunteers. He realized that he was unintentionally training volunteers to fail to return phone calls from him because they assumed he called only with bad news or complaints. He learned to follow a very simple (if inexact) formula for volunteer conversations. "Equal parts good news and bad news—we now want to stay out of the if-he's-calling-me-there-must-be-a-problem trap."

Loosigian now goes out of his way to contact volunteers with positive feedback. Loosigian or other staff at Exeter may, for example, call a class agent with the positive news that some of the agent's classmates attended a recent Exeter function. Or Loosigian will call to inform an agent that a recent phonathon or other class fund-raising event attracted 10 new donors, thereby adding to the class agent's fund-raising total. "I'll call to tell them a fund-raising letter they wrote is terrific," said Loosigian. "The simple act of engaging the volunteer in ongoing communication, in good and bad times, makes a huge difference in elevating their enthusiasm and their performance."

GETTING DOWN TO BUSINESS

The businesslike philosophy is apparent in program training materials that outline specific class fund-raising goals and even more specific volunteer job requirements. While each volunteer is issued a complete volunteer training manual, much of the information can now be accessed online, via the Exeter Web site (*www.exeter.edu*).

The Exonian class agent job description includes:

• Soliciting classmates for gifts to the Exeter Annual Giving Fund with calls, letters, and e-mails;

The Exeter Bulletin supports the work of academy volunteers by promoting class events and sustaining class relationships.

Class notes, written by volunteers, comprise two-thirds of each issue.

The Exeter Bulletin

Exonian reporters-at-large go in search of people with interesting stories to tell

SPRING 2000

Living in the Human
For the Good of the Te

PHILLIPS EXETER ACADEMY
20 MAIN STREET
EXETER, NEW HAMPSHIRE 03833-2460

It's Never Too Late for Reunions at Exeter

Reunion means something for everyone, especially the opportunity to recapture and reinvent the Exeter experience in your life today. It's not too late to register for your reunion this spring, and resume the Harkness discussions, continue the late-night debates, play another game of pick-up ball, or walk along the river—with partners and families, old friends and new.

REUNION DATE	YEAR	CLASS
April 28-30, 2000	60th	1940
	55th	1945
	45th	1955
	40th	1960
	35th	1965
May 5-7, 2000	25th	1975
May 12-14, 2000	30th	1970
	20th	1980
	15th	1985
	10th	1990
May 18-21, 2000	50th	1950
May 27-28, 2000	5th	1995

If you have questions or want to register, call Jan Woodford in the alumni/ae
affairs office at (603) 777-3474 or -3414; email jwoodford@exeter.edu

- Participating in local phonathons conducted by volunteers at locations around the country each year;

- Thanking donor classmates with personal notes, in addition to Exeter's own gift acknowledgements;

- Encouraging classmates to get involved in reunions and other Exeter events and volunteer opportunities; and

- Communicating regularly with the Exeter annual giving office about solicitation progress, address updates, and other information regarding class giving prospects.

The job description also mentions a required annual on-campus weekend of training and best practice sharing among volunteers. The get-together reinforces the program's roll-up-your-sleeves-and-get-to-work culture, with some class agents themselves serving as star experts. Some of Loosigian's favorites:

- The time-honored (although admittedly low-tech) example of the dog-eared class roster that Joe Bain, class agent for the Class of '41, proudly totes around. Each page of the roster is devoted to a classmate, and each entry includes extensive notes from Bain's contacts with the classmate and family and others close to the classmate. Bain even pastes updates from the periodic class notes he receives from Exeter on the classmate's page.

- The habit Kurt Perion, Class of '69, has of personalizing all mailings to classmates —even mass e-mailings. He'll take the extra time to cut and paste the body of an e-mail form letter into a message that contains a personal note for each classmate.

- The secret of success of many high-performing classes with multiple class agents lies in the regularly scheduled conference calls that update each agent's progress. These calls are managed by the agents themselves and may not involve Loosigian.

If all this sounds like best practice examples for a sales staff, it's no accident —it's just good business.

When Loosigian initially redefined the role of volunteers participating in the program and the goals they were expected to meet, the culture shift produced a few volunteer casualties. But Loosigian found that being upfront and clear went a long way toward minimizing potential hard feelings. "I have had volunteers who intended to do a good job but didn't commit the time we agreed to. More

Your Role as Class Agent

Each class agent has a special reason for volunteering for Phillips Exeter Academy. Some want to give back to the school that gave so much to them when they were students. Some like to stay in touch with classmates through personal contact of phonathons and solicitation notes. Some simply want to continue to be part of the school. There are probably as many reasons to volunteer as there are volunteers for Exeter, all of them important, both to the school and to the alumni/ae.

Whatever your reasons, bear in mind that you are key to the continued success of the school. The superb faculty, talented student body, beautiful campus – none of these can continue without the generous support of the alumni/ae. That support would be much less substantial without the determined efforts of class agents like you.

Class agents play a vital role in the Annual Giving Fund effort. You are the backbone of Phillips Exeter Academy's financial security and you are the Academy's most important link with its alumni/ae.

Please visit the Annual Giving web page at:

www.exeter.edu/alum/annualgiving.html

RESPONSIBILITIES

✓ Attend Alumni/ae Council Weekend at PEA each fall.

✓ Solicit classmates through verbal and written communication for contributions to the Annual Giving Fund.

✓ Encourage classmates to participate in Exeter activities, such as regional dinners and special events, and/or to visit the campus.

✓ Attend phonathons that take place near your home or work, AND recruit at least two classmates to participate in each phonathon located outside of your area.

✓ Maintain close communication, including information regarding top prospects, with the Annual Giving Office.

✓ Provide the Annual Giving Office with information about classmates concerning job changes, address and telephone changes for home and business, as well as marriages, births, deaths and general feelings about Exeter.

✓ Although all donors receive an acknowledgement from the Academy, class agents are encouraged to also call, write or e-mail a short note of thanks to their classmates. Postcards, notecards and stationery are available through the Annual Giving Office.

To register for a phonathon or to make a pledge on-line, go to the Quick Find box at the above address.

A class agent manual outlines specific responsibilities for volunteers, including time commitments and fund-raising goals. Many program-management functions are now handled online.

often than not, they would come to me disappointed and acknowledge that they weren't doing the job. We would disengage quietly, and I'd let them know that there were other ways for them to be involved."

A SELECT GROUP OF EXONIAN VOLUNTEERS

Not all volunteers possess identical skills. The academy's fund-raising growth for several years grew around the giving "spike" generated by class reunion-year campaigns that often trailed off in the years that followed. Class agents who challenged their top donor classmates to make significant reunion gifts were often unable to sustain or increase giving in non-reunion years.

Although grateful for the participation of all alumni volunteers, Loosigian recognized that a correlation usually existed between the size of gift being solicited and the amount of time required for cultivation and solicitation. "Some of our higher-end donors needed more cultivation than what the typical class agent was able to provide. The agents were being effective with most of their classmates— 95 percent of the class." That other five percent of the class, however, needed more focused attention than even the most accomplished class agent could provide. "We just needed another way to cultivate the major prospects."

In seeking another way, Loosigian looked again to his Exonian volunteers by forming a new leadership-giving group, The 1781 Society, to commemorate the year the school was founded. Membership in The 1781 Society requires a minimum annual gift of $1,781. Loosigian identified 42 volunteer solicitors primarily to solicit major prospects each year—prospects who are not participating in a class reunion that particular year. Although there might be more than 700 potential 1781 Society prospects in any given year, each volunteer receives a relatively light load of 10 prospects. As a result, volunteer solicitors can spend a manageable amount of time cultivating each of them.

Any prospects not assigned to a volunteer gift solicitor may, at Loosigian's discretion, be contacted by an experienced Exeter phonathon volunteer, an Exeter staff member, or, in the case of prospects who graduated before the early 1940s, simply a personal letter. Loosigian explained that Exeter alumni who graduated before 1940 are typically more responsive letters than to phone calls.

The creation of The 1781 Society and its own corps of volunteers was another shock for the Exonian volunteers. "That was another culture shift that some of

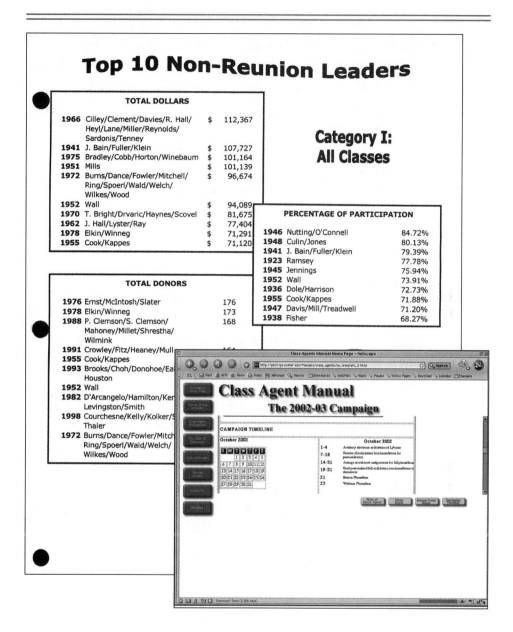

Top 10 Non-Reunion Leaders

TOTAL DOLLARS

1966	Cilley/Clement/Davies/R. Hall/ Heyl/Lane/Miller/Reynolds/ Sardonis/Tenney	$	112,367
1941	J. Bain/Fuller/Klein	$	107,727
1975	Bradley/Cobb/Horton/Winebaum	$	101,164
1951	Mills	$	101,139
1972	Burns/Dance/Fowler/Mitchell/ Ring/Spoerl/Wald/Welch/ Wilkes/Wood	$	96,674
1952	Wall	$	94,089
1970	T. Bright/Drvaric/Haynes/Scovel	$	81,675
1962	J. Hall/Lyster/Ray	$	77,404
1978	Elkin/Winneg	$	71,291
1955	Cook/Kappes	$	71,120

Category I: All Classes

PERCENTAGE OF PARTICIPATION

1946	Nutting/O'Connell	84.72%
1948	Culin/Jones	80.13%
1941	J. Bain/Fuller/Klein	79.39%
1923	Ramsey	77.78%
1945	Jennings	75.94%
1952	Wall	73.91%
1936	Dole/Harrison	72.73%
1955	Cook/Kappes	71.88%
1947	Davis/Mill/Treadwell	71.20%
1938	Fisher	68.27%

TOTAL DONORS

1976	Ernst/McIntosh/Slater	176
1978	Elkin/Winneg	173
1988	P. Clemson/S. Clemson/ Mahoney/Millet/Shrestha/ Wilmink	168
1991	Crowley/Fitz/Heaney/Mull	164
1955	Cook/Kappes	
1993	Brooks/Choh/Donohoe/Ea Houston	
1952	Wall	
1982	D'Arcangelo/Hamilton/Ker Levingston/Smith	
1998	Courchesne/Kelly/Kolker/S Thaler	
1972	Burns/Dance/Fowler/Mitch Ring/Spoerl/Wald/Welch/ Wilkes/Wood	

Class Agent Manual

The 2002-03 Campaign

CAMPAIGN TIMELINE

October 2002

Class fund-raising achievements and records are recognized and rewarded. Various class "categories" allow classes of similar ages to compete with each other. An online version of the training manual keeps volunteers informed about key program dates and activities.

our volunteers struggled with, no question. Class agents looked wounded when I told them that other volunteers would contact some of their classmates. Over time, though, they came to accept and embrace it," said Loosigian. He credits The 1781 Society "shift" for helping the Exeter Annual Giving program achieve its $5 million record in 2002.

AN INSTITUTION CREATES ITS OWN CULTURE

Phillips Exeter Academy fund raising took off when it decided to raise its expectations for volunteers. In regard to institutions that find mobilizing volunteers increasingly difficult, Loosigian wonders if they are focusing on the real problems. "I see other institutions that have volunteer structures, but I don't see all of them managing those structures as aggressively as they should. There's too much contentment on having 'bodies' on the committee," and not enough attention paid to the amount of time and work they offer or the results they produce.

It's important to note the deliberate things that Exeter does in support of its class-based fund-raising culture. Frequent alumni publications and events keep alumni thinking about Exeter in general and their former classmates in particular. Fully two-thirds of the content of the quarterly *Exeter Bulletin* (see page 77) consists of alumni class notes — written by other class volunteers. Referring back to the annual giving pyramid in the Introduction to this book (see page 3), it's easy to appreciate the strong foundations Exeter has built for sustaining Exonian affinity and instilling the philanthropic culture.

Few alumni wake up in the morning hoping that the alma mater will call to recruit them for volunteer fund-raising jobs. But the task of the annual giving program isn't to conclude that alumni *don't* want to be engaged. The challenge is to create a culture that invites alumni involvement, a culture that encourages volunteer satisfaction and fund-raising success. Whether your school uses class-based volunteers or some other kind of organization, Wayne Loosigian's volunteer management lesson is clear: Get down to business.

UNIVERSITY OF VIRGINIA: CLASS GIVING AT PUBLIC U

Reunion-based giving appeals are an important part of many college and university annual giving programs. For private schools like Phillips Exeter Academy, reunion giving programs are the centerpiece of annual giving efforts, with competition between classes each year inspiring volunteer involvement, increased alumni-giving participation, and record-breaking fund raising.

But when a public university embraces reunion giving, it's news. Public universities typically have large class sizes that diminish feelings of alumni class identity and undermine attempts at reunion-based giving. Instead, public universities often have colleges and other units with strong identities that receive priority through college- and department-based annual giving structures. The alumni office (or association) may still plan homecoming and reunion programs, but the central annual giving office may not get involved, concentrating instead on broad-based telemarketing and direct mail programs on behalf of its "client" schools and departments.

Historically, the University of Virginia's annual giving program was organized according to this structure. For many years, until the early '90s, UVA held annual homecoming events directed broadly to the entire alumni population. Because UVA has always enjoyed strong alumni affinity, reunion attendance was often good but lacked any strong connection with alumni giving.

Since 1999, however, UVA has held an annual spring reunion modeled on the private school five-year-anniversary-class format. During the reunion program's "high season," the central university staff recruits volunteers and schedules volunteer training weekends. Volunteers put together reunion-giving subcommittees, while the overall reunion chair focuses on programming activities. The overall reunion chair is recruited by the alumni association, and the annual giving staff recruits the class reunion-giving chair. In considering volunteers, the annual giving program looks at individuals' past involvement and volunteer time availability, as well as their giving capacity and ability to help expand the annual giving network by engaging new volunteers from their peer group.

Lots of private-school-like reunion giving competition has been introduced as well, including recognition listings for top class fund-raising performance. The alumni association offers a trophy for highest attendance, and the annual giving program presents awards for highest total giving and highest total class participation. The program has helped generate a competitive class spirit that the university did not actively cultivate in its students. Alumni may still lack strong class affiliations, but they still pull together and volunteer in response to the university's reunion challenge.

Class giving participation during reunions has increased, and reunion attendance has increased as well. But the program's real strength lies in attracting unusually large gifts from reunion alumni. Overall reunion giving has grown more than 70 percent—from $3.9 million in the program's first year (1999) to $5.6 million in 2002.

Several significant "spike" gifts were received during the years in between. In just the second year of the class reunion-giving program, the university received a $10 million gift tied to one donor's 25th reunion and a $2 million gift for another donor's 35th reunion. While UVA might have received those gifts anyway, staff credit the class reunion for giving donors additional motivation.

In one departure from the private school model, the UVA reunion-giving program continues to solicit alumni on behalf of the school from which they graduated. An annual report lists reunion class donors under the school they attended. In this way, the university is able to retain a school-based emphasis while using class reunion energy as a five-year tool to increase participation and overall fund raising.

The University of Virginia is a large school with, compared to most private schools, large class sizes. But the university is not prohibited from borrowing these traits it has in common with private schools—such as classmates' schools and years of attendance—that provide useful structures and approaches for fund raising. At UVA, alumni classmates don't need to know each other to work together to reach fund-raising goals in support of their alma mater.

Upgrading Leadership Donors

Acquiring many $1,000 annual fund donors is an achievement. Increasing their giving from there opens the door to major gift relationships

Many annual giving programs focus squarely on growing the number of donors each year. Their strategies tend to revolve primarily around broad solicitations—usually phonathons and large mailings—assuming that the more calls they make and the more letters they send, the more likely they are to reach their fund-raising goals by the end of the fiscal year.

As depicted by the annual giving pyramid in the Introduction to this book (see page 3), growing donor value is an important objective in its own right. At some point, annual giving programs should strive to identify not only an institution's supporters, but also those who are really interested in *philanthropy* and making larger gifts to the institution. In the same way that alumni, parents, and others can be taught the culture of gift support, the annual giving program can create a culture of leadership annual gift support. Are *you* teaching those who want to distinguish themselves as leadership supporters how to go about doing it?

Many schools use giving levels, or "societies," to encourage donors to make larger gifts and sustain their giving over a period of years. Often, these giving levels have a tiered structure of ascending "clubs" with specified annual donation levels, i.e., Century Club, $100; Dean's Circle, $250; Trustees' Society, $500, etc. With the University of Michigan's stewardship strategies, for example (see Chapter 8), new donors who contribute at certain giving levels receive special recognition and are more likely to feel involved in a long-term giving relationship.

CARNEGIE MELLON AT A GLANCE:

CARNEGIE MELLON UNIVERSITY Pittsburgh, Pennsylvania	
Nickname	Tartans
Type of institution	Private doctoral/ research university
Founded	1900
Total enrollment	8,588
Endowment market value	$667 million
Total alumni giving for current operations	$3,394,069
Undergraduate alumni of record	34,885
Graduate alumni of record	14,655
Alumni solicited	47,696
Alumni donors	12,047
Participation (of alumni solicited)	25%
Web site	www.carnegie.edu

POSITIONING THE ANDREW CARNEGIE SOCIETY

A "signature" leadership giving society at or near the top of this tiered ladder (usually at $1,000 and almost invariably named President's "Society" or "Circle") can provide a useful point of reference for donors who would like their annual gift to make a strong statement of support but don't know how much to contribute. Well-marketed, these leadership societies create cachet by providing donors with recognition (contributor listings and other prominent tributes), access (meetings and receptions with campus leaders), and campus "insider" status (often through periodic newsletters and memoranda from the president). As alumni become accustomed to the gratification they receive in exchange for their leadership donation and insider status, the hope is they will continue to contribute at that level.

This pleasant development can become a problem over time, however, as leadership societies succeed and donors get entrenched (or "plateaued" or "stuck") at a particular signature level. Frequently, much time and effort is spent recruiting membership into giving societies, but little thought goes into growth strategies

The Andrew Carnegie Society at Carnegie Mellon University was effective in attracting $1,000 donors. But where do they go from there?

beyond the President's Society-level gift. If the base amount for President's Society membership is $1,000 per year, that becomes the level where many members remain—unless they have an incentive to increase their gift. While many institutions create higher tiers above President's Society, it's hard to top the benefits that are typically offered at the signature $1,000 level. Often, little differentiates higher gift levels from the President's Society tier.

HIGH-END GIVING GAP

For Miriam Whitworth-Brown, director of annual giving at Carnegie Mellon University, the problem of plateaued donors emerged as she reviewed the membership roster of the Andrew Carnegie Society, a leadership (and notably non-presidentially named) donor giving society of Carnegie Mellon's annual giving program. "We were continuing to acquire new donors at the $1,000 level. From that standpoint, the program was achieving some primary objectives. However, we had developed a traffic jam at that level with no true structure in place to challenge [existing members] to do more."

While the number of $1,000 donors was growing, major gift officers faced a new problem. The minimum threshold for establishing an endowment had been increased from $25,000 to $50,000. This meant that it would cost a major gift prospect at least $50,000 to establish an endowment (a named scholarship, for example). If the pledge were extended over 10 years (the maximum pledge period allowed), a prospective donor would still have to make payments of at least $5,000 per year.

As a result, Carnegie Mellon had unintentionally created a gap in its giving marketing—or, looked at another way, in its line of giving "products." For the many donors whose giving had risen to $1,000 a year because of the Andrew Carnegie Society, the $5,000 per year required to endow a scholarship was a pretty big leap. And over shorter pledge periods, annual payments would be even higher.

"We didn't want to raise the $1,000 Andrew Carnegie Society threshold because we were still attracting new contributors," said Whitworth-Brown. "We'd worked hard to raise awareness of the Andrew Carnegie Society, and we felt we just needed a better way of moving our $1,000 donors toward major gift activity. We wanted to nudge their habits 'a little farther north.' We wanted to provide a giving opportunity for those donors who were capable of giving more than $1,000 per year. So, we thought about how to create a 'hybrid' program that bridged the gap between the $1,000 Andrew Carnegie Society threshold and the larger amounts necessary for endowed gifts."

THE MISSING LINK

What Carnegie Mellon came up with was the Legacy Scholarship Program of the Andrew Carnegie Society. Although the program had the look and feel of an endowment-giving program, it remained an initiative of the annual giving office because the funds it raised would be current-use operating dollars, not endowed funds for permanent scholarships.

The idea for the Legacy Scholarship Program emerged from a number of factors:

• **The giving range had to be relatively close to the $1,000 level.** In the same way that the university had succeeded in attracting so many $1,000 donors, Whitworth-Brown knew the new level needed to be reachable and durable. "In some ways, we knew we were establishing an important new threshold, one that could remain a focal point of the program for years." In the same way the university had succeeded with a "product" called the Andrew Carnegie Society, it now sought to launch a new product, the Legacy Scholarship Program. The annual giving staff homed in on the $2,500 level, an obvious in-between level that would allow donors to step up their giving without taking the giant leap to $5,000. But why would they want to?

- **A new and compelling reason for donors to increase their giving was required.** The Andrew Carnegie Society had been successfully marketed as a mechanism for demonstrating leadership-level support of the university. In fact, the program had been so well marketed that it suffered from a clustering of donors at the $1,000 threshold giving level. Andrew Carnegie Society donors viewed a $1,000 gift as a worthwhile investment, but they could not see any benefit to exceeding $1,000 — except going *far* above, to $5,000. The annual giving program had to provide a new incentive for its donors to give beyond the $1,000 Andrew Carnegie Society level.

- **What incentive could they offer?** "We thought about the existing benefits that donors receive when they endow the $50,000 scholarships through a major gift. Scholarship awards are made to students each year in the donor's name. The donor has the opportunity to meet and interact with the students who receive the scholarship award, and they almost always really value that sense of attachment to the educational work of the institution," said Whitworth-Brown. "The idea of the scholarships was also interesting to us, because aid for students could be raised and distributed as current-use funds. We saw potential for positioning the new program as similar to our endowed scholarship major gift program, but without the permanence." If it worked the way the annual giving staff envisioned, would the interaction with student scholarship recipients whet donors' appetites for future endowed major gifts?

- **Gifts needed to remain for current-use purposes.** It was imperative that, in providing an incentive for higher annual society membership gifts, the annual giving program did not step outside its own mission of providing the university with current-use operating funds. A scholarship program that applied annual funds directly to a student's tuition fit the definition. Every dollar raised through the Legacy Scholarship program would be available for current-use financial aid. The finance office was happy with the idea, and no obstacles remained to its implementation.

CAPACITY-BUILDING AT CARNEGIE MELLON

$1,000

**Andrew Carnegie
Society annual gift
amount**

$5,000

**Minimum annual
pledge payment for
a $50,000 endowed
fund**

While the Andrew Carnegie Society motivated gifts of $1,000, it created a big gap to overcome to motivate donors to make $5,000 endowment gifts.

A SOLUTION

$1,000

**Andrew Carnegie Society
annual gift amount**

$2,500

**Legacy Scholarship
Fund**

$5,000

**Minimum annual
pledge payment for
a $50,000 endowed
fund**

The Legacy Scholarship Program offered donors an in-between step — a $2,500 four-year pledge in exchange for a (temporarily) named scholarship.

MARKETING THE NEW PRODUCT

Legacy scholarships can be established with four annual payments of $2,500, a total commitment of $10,000. The scholarship is named in the donor's honor for those four years, and at the donor's request it can be designated for a student in a school or department. The donor receives recognition and personally meets the student recipient, who typically remains the recipient for the four years of the scholarship.

Because these scholarships are not endowed, legacy gifts provide immediate financial support in the first year. (In contrast, many endowed scholarship funds must accumulate interest earnings over a period of time before a first award can be made.) Upon completion of the four-year pledge, donor and student names are both inscribed on a commemorative plaque displayed on campus.

The concept was well received by donor prospects. "They now had the opportunity to experience a taste of life as a major donor and to meet students and feel more directly plugged into the educational life of the university," said Whitworth-Brown.

Equipped with this new vehicle for upgrading leadership donors, the Carnegie Mellon annual giving staff found a way to engage current $1,000 donors and generate results. From a total of seven $2,500 donors in 1998, the scholarship initiative increased to 38 $2,500 donors in 2000, most of them $1,000 contributors who had finally received an opportunity they could respond to. As the four-year giving period comes to an end, Carnegie Mellon then works to point Legacy Scholarship donors toward fully-endowed $50,000 scholarship funds.

For Carnegie Mellon, "the idea filled an important gap in our pipeline," said Whitworth-Brown. "For years we felt satisfied that we had giving levels for people to join, but we weren't using them as strategically as we could. The new scholarship program enabled us to address the donor capacity-building goals of the annual giving program and helped to bridge the giving gap with our major gift fund-raising programs as well."

Development offices are often guilty of establishing giving societies and endowment guidelines for their own internal reasons—including convenience. The perspective of the donor, as a result, can be overlooked. By thinking about the giving motivations of its donors and how well its giving "products" matched up with them, Carnegie Mellon created a new giving option that effectively expedited the progression from annual gift supporter to major gift philanthropist.

s e c t i o n 3

They Acquired Better Knowledge

Donor Retention Through Data Mining

A close examination of past giving trends mandated an all-out
campaign to forge long-term relationships with first-year donors

L earning from past efforts is an important part of annual giving program
planning. By looking at the giving data from donor constituencies, you
learn about their giving trends and tendencies, information that permits
you to implement strategies that take advantage of the opportunities their habits
present for fund-raising growth.

While annual giving directors often rush to implement strategies and programs in response to reported *national* demographic shifts and changes, the *best*
program changes are often those implemented in response to what they've
learned about the giving habits and tendencies of their *own* donor audience.

A DESIRE TO DO MORE

The University of Michigan annual giving program, like most programs, identifies
alumni-giving participation as a goal. In seeking to maximize alumni participation, though, the U-M annual giving program staff understood the value of breaking participation into component parts. They began by dividing the participation
goal into three key groups:

- **Donor** *retention*—number of existing donors who will continue to give
  this year

MICHIGAN AT A GLANCE:

UNIVERSITY OF MICHIGAN Ann Arbor, Michigan	
Nickname	Wolverines
Type of institution	Public doctoral/ research university
Founded	1817
Total enrollment	53,031
Endowment market value	$3.45 billion
Total alumni giving for current operations	$25,952,214
Alumni of record	412,148
Alumni solicited	386,744
Alumni donors	61,805
Participation (of alumni solicited)	16%
Web site	www.umich.edu

- **Donor *reactivation***—number of former donors who will resume giving this year

- **Donor *acquisition***—number of new donors who will give for the first time this year

The annual giving staff then developed specific strategies for approaching each donor group. By tracking the results for each strategy over time, they identified specific activities that could have significant impact on achieving their overall alumni participation goals.

For Julie Brown, the University of Michigan annual giving program director, operational strategies usually require subdividing these groups even further. "Our reactivation strategies look at approaches for the short-lapsed (only one or two years since last gift), long-lapsed (three to six years), and super-lapsed (seven years and up). We then tailor phrases in letter copy and talking points for Telefund [phonathon] scripts for these specific audiences. For example, short-lapsed donors are more likely to read references to their last gift. The super-lapsed donors, by comparison, are not."

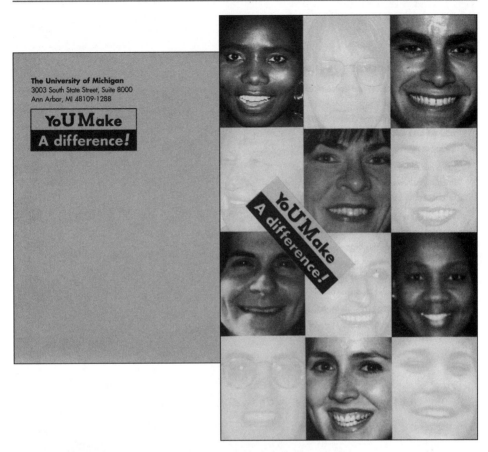

Michigan's first new-donor appreciation mailing emphasized the value of every gift and sent Rolodex cards to facilitate communication with the university.

By coding and tracking the gifts it receives from each segment, the U-M learns things. "Our super-lapsed prospects almost always perform better than our non-donors," said Brown. "My guess previously would have been that there was little difference between our super-lapsed donors and our non-donors. Now, when we need to prioritize how we spend our budget dollars, I know I'm likely to raise more through one more mailing to the super-lapsed donors than from a mailing to non-donors."

WHERE TO DIG FOR DATA

In learning about the relative impact on each group's overall participation rate, the U-M annual giving staff worked with their in-house database and computer programming staff to develop reports that tracked the program's success in achieving its yearly retention, reactivation, and acquisition goals.

"We spent several years developing a donor retention report, something that showed us what donors we were keeping and in what categories," said Brown. "We needed to know if we were keeping a loyal core of donors and moving them up the giving ladder, or if we were simply replacing old donors with new donors each year. After several attempts, we got the report the way we wanted it. This allowed us to emphasize end-of-the-year appeals and warn school development officers if they had significant annual donors who had not renewed their gifts."

Brown also began to use an outside vendor's statistical tabulating service to elicit additional detail about the giving trends and habits of the university's alumni donor audience. When several other Big Ten schools began use the same reports, the data became even more valuable. "It was very helpful to see our data analyzed by an impartial vendor and then to see our results compared with some of our peers'. This helped us see where we were strong and where we were weak in comparison to other large public university programs with similar challenges and constituencies," said Brown.

Since Michigan solicits hundreds of thousands of alumni each year, there is much to admire in the staff's ability to simply *manage* such an enormous program. Having good data, though, enabled Brown and her staff to think beyond the *process* of solicitation and delve into strategy issues. For starters, the staff noted that the university was retaining 68 percent of its donors from year to year.

It's hard to effectively discuss annual giving strategy in the absence of data—yet many schools do. The University of Michigan and others increasingly use a combination of internal reports and external vendor data analysis to track many alumni-giving trends, including:

- Percentage of donors retained
- Average gift per retained donor
- Percentage of lapsed donors reactivated
- Average gift per reactivated donor
- Number of new donors
- Average gift per new donor
- Percentage of donors who increase or decrease their giving each year
- Number of donors lost last year
- Gift dollars lost last year
- Alumni-giving percentage
- Donors by giving level

- Donors by years of giving
- First-time donor retention
- Lapsed donor reactivation rates by number of years lapsed
- Average gift by previous years of giving
- Giving by appeal
- Giving by gender
- Giving by school
- Giving by class
- Gifts per donor
- Total number of donors
- Total gift revenue

While this was slightly higher than the Big Ten average, the staff set an overall donor-retention goal of 70 percent. What new strategies would be required to retain seven of every 10 contributors in the coming year? And if they hit 70 percent, could the program retain an even higher percentage in years to come?

Further analysis indicated that the annual giving program was doing an excellent job of retaining multiyear donors, recording an 87 percent retention rate for donors of five consecutive years or more. However, the program was failing to retain an alarming number of first-year contributors.

"When we looked at the report it was fairly clear that the regular donors were coming back at a decent clip, but it was the first-year people where we had the significant drop-off," said Brown. Only 36 percent of the donors who made their first gift to the university went on to make a second gift the following year. Because attracting new donors is among the most costly components of any

Michigan is one of the great institutions of higher learning in the world, and its greatness is in no small measure due to your loyalty, your affection and your generosity. Your appreciation for the University of Michigan, your recognition of its value in your own life and its future value in the lives of so many others, and your willingness to share your resources on its behalf, bode well for its continued well being and for the futures of all of us.

Lee C. Bollinger
President
University of Michigan

Thank You!

Your gift to your schools' Annual Fund does make a difference! Michigan students and faculty depend on the generosity of alumni/ae now more than ever. Most University gifts are earmarked, and must be spent on specific projects. Discretionary Annual Fund dollars provide the Dean and directors of your school with the flexibility to fund new initiatives or to respond quickly to emergency situations. Annual Fund gifts greatly enhance the excellence of a Michigan education.

Yo**U M**ake a Difference!

Welcome Aboard!

We welcome your support and encourage you to stay connected to Michigan.

- Use our bookmark for the *Giving To Michigan* web address and visit our site to learn more about philanthropy at Michigan.

- Keep our Alumni-Donor Help Line phone card handy in case you have questions about your alumni record or about your University gift, pledge or receipt.

- If you aren't a member already, consider joining thousands of your fellow alumni/ae as a member of the Alumni Association. This organization provides Michigan alumni/ae with a wide variety of programs. New services include internet access through Michigan OnLine and an online alumni directory.

- Finally, we hope you will enjoy and display with pride our non-permanent cling block M decal.

Stay Connected!

VISIT THE NEW GIVING TO THE UNIVERSITY OF MICHIGAN WEBSITE WHERE YOU'LL FIND: http://www.giving.umich.edu

- Q&A About Giving. A compendium of questions most asked by donors.
- Gifts Make a Difference. The impact of private gifts on the University's long tradition of excellence.
- How to Make a Gift. Your guide to gift-making with forms, instructions, tax information and more.
- Opportunities for Personal Giving. The many ways your gift can make a difference.
- Corporate and Foundation Relations. Information of interest to our corporate and foundation partners.
- Development Programs & People. University staff who can help you make your gift the way a gift is recognized.

The new-donor appreciation mailing did what was previously unthinkable in the annual giving office: It encouraged alumni to become dues-paying members of Michigan's alumni association. A bookmark introduced the university's new Web site.

fund-raising program, the low retention rates for first-time donors made U-M's cost effectiveness even worse. Lots of effort went into *attracting* new donors, but not enough effort went into *keeping* them.

Additionally, the report revealed that first-year donors who made a second gift in the second year were much more likely to contribute in the third year and beyond. A second gift was a critical barometer of the university's ability to form a giving relationship with a donor, and first-year donor retention was clearly dragging down the university's overall 68 percent donor retention rate.

Information like this is vital because sustaining contributors is critical to the cost-effectiveness of any annual giving program. Once donor loyalty has been established, the cost of fund raising for retained donors drops to a fraction of the cost of acquiring new contributors. "Our high-end donor renewal mailing, which goes to our multiyear donors, usually has a $.04 to $.05 cost per dollar raised, while we are lucky to break even (like most schools) on most of our non-donor mailings," Brown explained. In fact, the unappreciated silver lining for most successful annual giving programs is the reliable revenue stream from loyal donors who steadily increase their gifts over time.

Having established that the poor retention of first-year contributors was weighing down its overall alumni-giving participation rate, the U-M annual giving staff decided that first-year contributors deserved (or sorely needed) special attention. For an annual giving program that historically acknowledged all contributors in largely the same manner, this concept mandated special changes to the existing program.

TIME FOR A CHANGE

Armed with data, Brown explored possible changes to the current program. "We said, 'All right, what are we going to do about these people, how can we focus in on these donors, and what kinds of things can we put together to try to get more of them coming back as donors again?'"

Brown identified several broad goals for U-M First Time Donors (FTDs):

- Broaden the base of alumni donors to the university by increasing the FTD giving renewal rate.

- Increase awareness of the annual fund's importance and the ongoing importance of gifts from FTDs and lapsed donors.

- Improve retention with FTDs by emphasizing their participation at *any* level, not just with increased gifts.

- Thank first-time donors for their annual fund contributions in a meaningful way by helping them feel an ongoing connection to the institution.

For lessons on how to increase donor retention, they first looked to arts and cultural institutions. With no alumni-like attachments automatically felt by their prospect audiences, arts organizations long ago learned the importance of making

The 2002 version of the new-donor welcome mailing included a CD-ROM with up-to-date information about the university and a virtual campus tour.

their supporters feel like "members" who enjoyed an established and ongoing relationship with the institution. For a university annual giving program that viewed each year as a campaign beginning anew, such thinking was new and unfamiliar.

To begin with, the U-M annual giving staff created a special "Welcome Aboard" package for first-year contributors. This mailing was separate from the official gift receipt and any acknowledgement letter that the school receiving the gift might have sent. Beginning with a bright yellow envelope bearing a bold "Thank You," the package included several "get-connected" items:

- **Acknowledgment brochure.** Headlined "Welcome Aboard," it urged first-time donors to "stay connected," stressing the importance of the gift and the difference the donor was making for the university. It also suggested that, if not already a member, the donor should join the alumni association.

- **Rolodex cards.** Cards contained contact information for the U-M "donor help line," the alumni association, development office, and other campus entities.

- **Bookmark.** Copy on bookmark encouraged donors to visit the U-M Web site to find answers to common donor questions, information on the impact and uses of private gifts, and instructions for making their next gift online.

- **Block M window decal.** The bold decal allowed them to display their pride and support of the university.

Each month a file was generated with data on all the new donors, and the mailing envelopes were laser printed. Telefund clerks stuffed the packages and mailed them first class. "We mailed between 300 and 1,200 each month, depending upon the time of year and the solicitation schedule. The budget averaged around $4,000 for a year, depending upon the need to reprint supplies," said Brown. To keep costs down, nothing was personalized except the mailing envelope.

NEW LOVE FOR NEW DONORS

"We knew right away the package got noticed," Brown related. "One of our high-end annual donors jokingly complained that his buddy at work 'got this really neat package' for his first-time gift, and the regular donor wanted to know what he was going to get."

Another important part of the project was to establish a system that consistently identified donors who met the first-time donor criteria. A new, distinct

As first-time donor retention has increased...

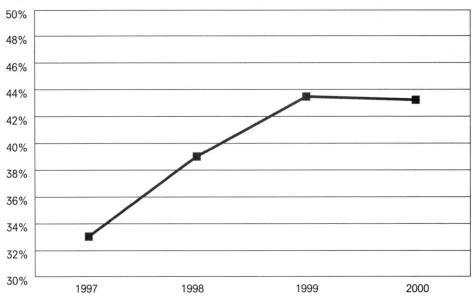

Percentage of First-Year Donors Retained

...overall retention has increased.

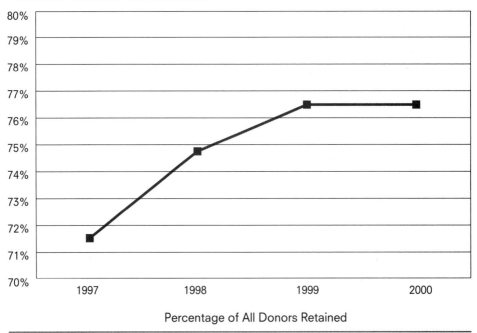

Percentage of All Donors Retained

code was created on the database that automatically identified first timers and flagged them for special treatment in all solicitations for the coming year. In the telemarketing program, for example, a special code appeared on the screen to alert the student caller. Students were trained to emphasize the *renewal* of the donor's gift as opposed to pushing for an *increased* amount. "We needed to establish the pattern of giving to Michigan. In another year we can go after the upgrade," said Brown.

Direct mail copy was also tailored to first-year donors. Letters would thank the donors for their first gifts during the previous fiscal year and encourage them to continue the tradition. And since the annual giving staff felt these "at risk" contributors needed another ask to make the case for renewal, they added an extra mailing in late February directed specifically to the first-year donor audience. There was a natural opening at this time in the pattern of asks for the year — right after the end of calendar year gifts were counted and before the fiscal year end push began. "We wanted to give them an extra opportunity to remember Michigan," said Brown.

Progress was made. In the four years since the first-year donor retention effort started, the percentage of second-year donors retained grew to more than 42 percent. Julie Brown was pleased that the U-M annual giving program was able to learn from its own history. "We saw growth in the overall number of alumni donors as well as dollars, and this program helped make that happen. We got smarter about learning from our own donor data. Once we could see where the opportunities were, we were able to design strategies that would help us reach our donor retention and participation goals."

Most college and university databases contain a wealth of knowledge that can help annual giving officers grow their programs. It is vital for annual giving officers to learn how to access this data, analyze and interpret it, and develop appropriate solicitation strategies and programs. Careful testing and tracking will enable development strategists to maximize donor participation and increase annual giving revenues. Your donors tell you something every time they make a gift. It is your responsibility to learn from their giving records so you can help to maximize their relationship with your institution.

DONOR RECOGNITION SOCIETIES

Donor giving societies have become so commonplace in annual giving programs that a school would be conspicuous if it didn't have any. Donor giving societies have almost always been used to recognize ascending levels of giving and motivate donors to progressively increase gift amounts over time.

As the University of Michigan discovered, a donor's long-term *loyalty* can be just as valuable as the amount of the yearly gift. Yet, schools have been slow to recognize and reward donors for longevity. They are quick to recognize total lifetime giving *amounts*, but slow to recognize a *lifetime of giving*. What's more, if the goal is to encourage stronger donor loyalty and affinity, shouldn't recognition for loyalty be as prominent as giving-amount-based societies?

Things have started to change. Here are donor recognition societies that reward donor loyalty, instead of the size of the gift:

- **Pennsylvania State University:** The *Golden Lion Society* offers membership only to those Penn State alumni who give each and every year after their graduation. In 2002, 14,000 alumni qualified.

- **Bradley University:** Any donor who has contributed for three or more consecutive years qualifies for the *Bradley Pride Society*.

- **Virginia Tech University:** The *Pylon Society* recognizes donors starting at the fifth consecutive year of giving, with additional tiered levels and benefits at 15 and 25 years.

Learning About Alumni

The Cal Fund conducted market research on its alumni to learn why they give—and why they don't

Anyone who has managed an annual giving program can tell you that they spend a lot of time on process: making sure phonathon pledge cards get printed, making sure appeal mailings reach the post office on schedule, and making sure all volunteers get training kits (not to mention training) for the upcoming reunion-giving program.

In this whirlwind of activity, it's no surprise when key decisions about annual giving message points get lost in the shuffle. You've gone to the trouble of recruiting students for the phonathon, but who's got time to think about what you want them to *say*? The production of your year-end mailing is behind schedule (and consequently at risk of becoming a year-*beginning* letter), so why not use the letter text from last year? (What did it say last year, anyway?)

The annual giving director often functions as plant manager, ensuring that all the annual giving appeal-manufacturing processes are on time and on budget. Often overlooked are fundamental questions about why you deserve the donors' support—your giving case for support.

While organizations like CASE help schools share sample appeal letters, brochures, phonathon scripts, and other solicitation materials, decisions about an annual giving program's best case for support are often driven by a run-with-the-pack mentality: "Our brochure/letter/phonathon script reads like most everyone else's brochure/letter/phonathon script, so it must be good enough."

UC, BERKELEY AT A GLANCE:

UNIVERSITY OF CALIFORNIA, BERKELEY Berkeley, California	
Nickname	Golden Bears
Type of institution	Public doctoral/ research university
Founded	1850
Total enrollment	32,128
Endowment market value	$1.774 billion
Total alumni giving for current operations	$22,475,428
Undergraduate alumni of record	223,818
Graduate alumni of record	74,605
Alumni solicited	296,063
Alumni donors	29,569
Participation (of alumni solicited)	10%
Web site	www.berkeley.edu

Even worse, annual giving programs often base decisions on a few odd phonathon comments or remarks from alumni. I've often heard annual giving directors declare mailings/brochures/scripts/etc. successful because of the "many positive remarks" they received. The reverse, of course, occurs just as often. Strategies are abandoned because of a few angry e-mails or phone call hang ups—and woe to the annual giving director who must answer for a complaint that comes into the president's office.

This isn't to say that all decisions based on this anecdotal evidence wind up being wrong. It's just that these decisions are often based on incomplete information. As someone smart once said, "The plural of anecdote is not data." Too many incorrect conclusions are drawn from alumni remarks that don't necessarily reflect the whole. In addition, the conclusions are often imprecise. If an alumnus says, "Don't ever call me again," is he/she objecting to the phone call, the institution, the timing, or innumerable other factors? What's really going on?

DESIRE FOR DATA

Few annual giving programs had ever set out to learn the true giving motivations of their own alumni in a statistically reliable, non-anecdotal way. The University of California, Berkeley, is one that did.

Like many annual giving programs, Berkeley's Cal Fund solicits gifts for unrestricted purposes; gifts to the Cal Fund can be used for any priority the university identifies. This creates both a marketing challenge and an opportunity. If gifts benefit the university in a broad, general way, what does that leave us to talk about *specifically*?

I've seen many annual giving letters attempt to tackle this, often with painful results. They explain how annual fund gifts help to pay the light bill or the snowplow bill. "Unglamorous," the letters say, "but necessary." And uninspiring. So many exciting things happen at your institutions every day. They are gift-wrapped for you to talk about them. Which will excite a would-be donor?

In 2001, the University of California, Berkeley Foundation (UCBF) identified alumni annual giving as one of its top fund-raising priorities. With advance discussions of a university-wide capital campaign in the works, the UCBF board wanted to increase alumni-giving participation in the months leading up to the campaign. A staff and board annual funds marketing committee was formed that, as one of its first action items, recommended that reliable market research should guide enhancements to the annual giving program.

The committee's objectives were twofold. First, learn about the drivers and deterrents of alumni giving—in other words, what motivates alumni to give and what makes them decide *not* to give. Second, use the research to guide decision making for the overall annual giving program. Should all alumni be solicited the same way?

MECHANICS OF MARKET RESEARCH

Market research helps annual giving programs make informed fund-raising strategy decisions. For many programs, research too often consists simply of looking at what peer institutions are doing or basing decisions on anecdotes that may or may not be representative of the entire prospect audience. It typically combines some *qualitative* research elements (i.e., by talking to a handful of *representative* alumni at length, can we identify and explore giving issues?) as well as *quantitative* (i.e., can we survey *enough* people so that the issues identified can be confirmed with the larger alumni audience?) Used in tandem, the two approaches offer a statistically valid sample method of gathering alumni opinions.

Focus groups are one method of gathering qualitative information about reasons for alumni support. Typically held with groups of eight to 12 alumni, focus groups are facilitated discussions about a short list of topics—in this case the annual giving program's case for support. Although the responses from focus group participants cannot be used to determine what the *entire* alumni population might say, the results are useful in identifying key thoughts and issues that can fine-tune questions in an alumni survey.

Following focus groups, a broader survey instrument is needed to gather information from a larger group of alumni. This process uses a more rigid series of questions typically asked in phone interviews, mail surveys, and, increasingly, e-mail surveys.

Responsibility for Berkeley's first foray into alumni giving market research fell into the hands of Lishelle Blakemore, director of annual giving, and Laurent (Lo) De Janvry, associate director of annual programs. In an unusual instance of Bay Area esprit de corps between rival institutions, Blakemore and De Janvry sought guidance for their research process from Jerold Pearson, a full-time alumni relations and development market researcher at Stanford University. Pearson had conducted a number of market research studies with Stanford alumni and the alumni of other college and university clients. (Pearson's Web site—*www.stanford.edu/~jpearson*—summarizes information about several of his studies.)

Initial focus group conversations with alumni had suggested key themes in alumni-giving decision making. Pearson then helped craft a survey that was used for telephone interviews with several hundred Berkeley alumni. The questions explored and tested many different assumptions about alumni opinions and attitudes toward Berkeley, reactions to different reasons why alumni support the university, and reasons why alumni chose not to support. A professional telephone survey company conducted these interviews over a three-week period.

Because Berkeley knew the general demographic characteristics of alumni who were being surveyed (particularly their age), the university could see similarities and differences among different groups once it sorted and analyzed the responses.

WHY ALUMNI GIVE (AND WHY THEY DON'T)

UC Berkeley's market research provided useful insights about why alumni give to the Cal Fund. While some presumed motivations for giving resonated, it was surprising to see which motivations did not. Blakemore and De Janvry divided the two types of motivations into *Drivers*—arguments that have motivating value with alumni—and *Dogs*—arguments that did not (see page 112). Among their findings:

- **UC Berkeley alumni favor supporting individual people through their giving.** This suggests that the Cal Fund should emphasize how gifts fund scholarships and provide other direct students benefits.

- **UC Berkeley alumni did not feel a particularly strong indebtedness or personal responsibility for supporting Cal.** The Cal Fund was going to have to provide more compelling reasons and evaluate how to impact this absence of a giving culture over the longer term.

- **Alumni in general enjoyed hearing from students about the case for gift support.** Although, notably, older alumni preferred instead hearing from the chancellor. This reaffirmed the value of using the phonathon for direct interaction between UC Berkeley students and alumni.

Just as revealing were the valuable insights into why alumni *don't* support the Cal Fund. It was important to learn that the best arguments for making a gift can be undermined by alumni feelings that cause them to not make a gift. Some key deterrents to giving included:

- **Gifts to other organizations had more significant impact.** Berkeley alumni thought that smaller, needier organizations would benefit more significantly from a gift. How could Berkeley make prospective donors realize that their gifts were valued — and valuable?

- **Berkeley's use of Cal Fund gifts was not well known.** Alumni felt inadequately informed about how their gifts were being used. Could Berkeley provide a better accounting?

- **Their relationship with Berkeley was no longer strong.** Older alumni, especially, expressed apathetic feelings toward the university. While the Cal Fund staff felt limited in its ability to resuscitate alumni affinity, the finding raised important alumni relations/annual giving program issues. If alumni relations programs can keep alumni involved, will annual giving program benefit?

BERKELEY'S "DRIVERS"

Giving arguments that resonate with Berkeley alumni

- Giving to Cal is a way to help students.
- State funding cuts have made alumni support more important.
- Giving helps Berkeley's research positively impact the world.
- Alumni support helps Cal attract the best faculty and students.
- Gifts enable the university to fund innovative programs.

BERKELEY'S "DOGS"

Giving arguments that did not resonate with Berkeley alumni

- I feel a sense of responsibility.
- I owe something in return.
- I want to give something back.
- The value of my degree depends on Cal's strength and my giving.
- Alumni giving impacts Cal's rankings in publications.
- My gift supports the chancellor's vision and goals.

BERKELEY'S "HIDDEN DOGS"

Arguments *against* giving that cause Berkeley alumni to choose *not* to make a gift

- Cal doesn't need my money as much as other organizations do.
- My gift has a greater impact on smaller and local organizations.
- I don't know where my gift dollars go or how they are used.

- **They suspected that gifts to Berkeley were somehow wasted.** Younger alumni, in particular, expressed concern that the university was too large to use their gifts meaningfully.

THE IMPACT

Once the Cal Fund staff had the research data, it began to consider opportunities to refine its appeals. Among the changes:

- **Appeal messages emphasize Berkeley's impact on individuals, particularly students.** Brochures feature photos of students, as opposed to institutional elements like buildings.

- **Follow-up accounting to donors has increased.** "We do an increased job of letting donors know how their gifts are appreciated, and how the Cal Fund is benefiting our students throughout the year. E-mail has been a particularly useful tool in this regard," said Blakemore.

- **Renewed emphasis has been placed on student-driven phonathon solicitation.** "We need to remind alumni of their time here and continue to grow the culture of alumni gift support. A nice conversation with a Berkeley student helps to send a lot of messages that we're trying to get across — that alumni and students are all part of a Berkeley community, that students are following in their footsteps today, and that lots of alumni choose to support us," said Blakemore.

While many annual giving programs will continue to base planning decisions on anecdotes and "what's going on elsewhere," the UC Berkeley survey process has helped it learn about its own particular alumni audience. Just as UC Berkeley has long been a leader in academic research, its annual giving office has proven conclusively that the plural of anecdote is *still* not data.

A Strategic Plan for Annual Giving

In seeking to improve yearly fund-raising totals,
USC mapped a vision for its annual fund future

A nnual giving programs often represent a paradox to the people who run them. The time commitment involved in orchestrating mailings, telemarketing, volunteers, and other details often precludes opportunities for strategic planning and other forms of forward thinking. Just when programs have achieved their annual goals and you have a moment to catch your breath, the immediate need arises to match (or exceed!) last year's amount. It's time to get the year's kickoff mailing designed…and in the mail…and on and on.

Yet, with ever-changing methods and media, perhaps no component of a university's fund-raising enterprise is more in need of continual updating and review than the annual giving program. With the Internet, telemarketing, direct mail, personal solicitation, and other viable solicitation alternatives weighing in, a written plan for the annual giving program is more essential now than ever. Unfortunately, due to time constraints and other aspects of the program that frequently absorb a director of annual giving's immediate attention, formal planning doesn't always happen.

UNIVERSITY OF SOUTHERN CALIFORNIA Los Angeles, California	
Nickname	Trojans
Type of institution	Private doctoral/ research university
Founded	1880
Total enrollment	28,154
Endowment market value	$2.13 billion
Total alumni giving for current operations	$12,839,234
Alumni of record	168,760
Alumni solicited	167,530
Alumni donors	42,232
Participation (of alumni solicited)	25%
Web site	www.usc.edu

WHAT'S A STRATEGIC PLAN?

While no excess of plan writing occurs in annual giving, there is plenty of variety in the types of plans. A tip of my hat goes to those annual giving programs that manage to prepare a durable operating plan each year. *Operating plans* typically focus on the current program year, detailing specific goals along with the quantifiable objectives and tactics that will be used to accomplish the goals. The many varieties of operating plans include plans that detail specifics on day-to-day timing of tactics and activities, respective staff responsibilities, and the budget costs for each activity—often accompanied with revenue projections. (For an example of one operating plan, see box about McKendree College on page 126.)

Much rarer than an operating plan is an annual giving *strategic plan,* a longer-perspective vision that often extends five years out or more. A strategic plan looks at the big picture to determine where the program is and where the program's trying to go.

WHY HAVE A STRATEGIC PLAN?

Before you reject strategic planning as another useless, irrelevant bureaucratic exercise, consider the benefits of a well-constructed annual giving plan:

- **It organizes activity.** Effective annual giving is as much about organization as it is about anything else. "I've been in annual fund drives where you just move from one crisis to the next," said Mary Rundus, the director of annual funds and grants at Westminster College in Fulton, MO. "With so many details to cover, a planning process lets us map everything out at the beginning."

Once the annual giving staff takes time to thoughtfully map out the program's goals, strategies, methods, budgets, and timelines, it has armed itself with a stress-reducing point of reference. "We're not perfect at this yet," Rundus added, "but even when things do get off course, the plan helps us to refocus and get back on track."

- **It puts the program in a larger context.** Is the annual giving program responsible for increasing the number of $1,000 leadership annual donors in advance of a major capital campaign? Does the college president want alumni-giving participation to increase by 20 percent over the next five years? A strategic plan addresses issues like these and makes the annual giving program function as part of a larger whole.

- **It builds awareness among internal and external audiences.** A strategic plan can educate both administrators and volunteer leaders about the annual fund's role and purpose in the organization at the same it shows how well it's performing. Don't expect people to be excited about the growth of your donor retention rate, for instance, if you have not taken the time to explain what it is, why it's important thing, and how it compares to your current goal and past achievements.

- **It's a useful evaluation tool.** A good strategic plan can be pulled from the drawer and used as a periodic measure of program evaluation for as long as it's intended. To annual giving programs driven by the urgent and the immediate, a strategic plan can offer a good perspective on how well the program is performing over the longer term.

- **It provides continuity.** "Talented annual giving people tend to be in demand, and they have a lot of opportunities to go elsewhere," said Ron Stephany, vice president for university relations at the University of Redlands in Redlands, CA. High staff turnover can deplete institutional memory, leaving today's staff to wonder what the previous staff was thinking. As a result, annual giving programs are perpetually rebuilding.

A written strategic plan expresses the long-term vision and thinking of the people who created it. As Stephany puts it, Redlands' annual giving plan "can steady our ship if we have a staff loss." Staffers who move on can thus leave a legacy greater than a stack of undialed phonathon pledge cards.

At the University of Southern California, a strategic plan grew out of concern for the performance of the annual giving program. In the years prior to creating a plan, the program suffered from uneven fund-raising results, inconsistent alumni-giving patterns, an internal and external identity crisis, and a feeling of falling behind due to changes in technology, alumni demographics and lifestyles, and communications preferences. Having had three annual giving directors in five years, the program lacked both continuity and a written roadmap for the future.

USC'S STRATEGIC "PLAN BLUEPRINT"

1. GOALS
- **Annual Giving Program Mission:**
  Maximize gift income annually from alumni, students, and friends
- **Goal 1:** Build compelling case for annual support of the university
- **Goal 2:** Achieve 30 percent alumni participation in three years
- **Goal 3:** Help to guide university-wide annual giving marketing plan
- **Goal 4:** Set foundation for even stronger future growth beyond three years

2. KEY INTERNAL OBSERVATIONS
- Increasing appeal costs
- Inconsistent alumni giving patterns
- Low internal identity of USC Annual Fund
- Low alumni-giving culture and USC Annual Fund identity
- Inadequate data and no dialogue with peer schools

3. KEY EXTERNAL TRENDS
- Increased giving competition from other not-for-profits
- Increased prominence of *U.S. News & World Report*-type rankings
- Lifestyle changes altering alumni interests
- Technology changes altering alumni communication and banking methods

4. SOLUTIONS – CREATING CORE COMPETENCIES

Initiatives identified over the following three years in four areas:

- **MARKETING, ADVERTISING, AND PROGRAMMING**

  Create new internal and external identity for annual giving with:
  - Dialogue between schools
  - Strong central office leadership
  - Central coordination of appeals
  - Coordinated stewardship programs
  - New advertising campaigns
  - New annual giving logo
  - Increased market research
  - Statistical analysis
  - Demographic giving trends
  - Appeal segment testing
  - Maximizing results of current efforts
  - Revised and simplified mailing schedule
  - Increased telemarketing fulfillment
  - Investigating new program ideas
  - Matching gift challenge
  - Multiple-year pledges
  - Improved donor stewardship

- **STRATEGIC ALLIANCES**

  Partner with the alumni association
  - Teach students about giving
  - Recruit and educate alumni leaders
  - Promote alumni association membership

  Partner with the units
  - Coordinate a master reunion calendar
  - Provide customized appeals for units

- **RESEARCH, TECHNOLOGY, AND DATABASE**

  Research
  - Review peer programs
  - Develop comparison benchmarks

  Technology
  - Install toll-free donor number
  - Online giving capability
  - Electronic funds transfer

  Database
  - Purge older non-donor records
  - Improve data cleanup processes
  - Store alumni survey data online

- **ORGANIZATION, STAFFING, AND INFRASTRUCTURE**
  - Provide ongoing staff training
  - Integrate functions between offices
  - Incrementally add staff
  - Offer orientation of new alumni-board annual giving
  - Create internal annual giving advisory board
  - Exchange best practices ideas between units

5. LINKING WITH ANNUAL OPERATING PLANS

- What are the incremental alumni participation goals for this year?
- What initiatives within each core competency should be accomplished this year?
- What are the budget and staffing implications for this year?
- What is the timeline and calendar for this year?
- When will the next review and evaluation of the strategic plan occur?
- Do we need to make any adjustments to the strategic plan?
- Are we still on course?

It is said that effective goal *getting* results from effective goal *setting*. For Jennifer Houlihan Warwick, the USC annual giving director, that meant embarking on a planning process that involved examining issues and trends, and identifying changes that would point the program in the right direction.

WHAT ARE WE TRYING TO ACCOMPLISH?

The most important part of a strategic plan is the explanation of what it is trying to accomplish. It should be produced with input that extends well beyond the annual giving office itself. What are the institution's long-term fund-raising goals? Is a capital campaign lurking on the horizon? Do you need to develop a stronger alumni-giving culture? How does the annual giving office collaborate with the alumni relations program and other campus offices? In your efforts to raise more funds, do you need to build a new way of going about it?

USC sought to create a "successful standard-setting annual fund-raising program." By its own definitions, that meant:

- Creating a compelling case for annual support of the university;

- Providing leadership by guiding an effective university-wide integrated marketing plan for annual support that engaged and involved fund raising, university relations, and alumni programming staff;

- Reaching 30 percent undergraduate alumni participation; and

- Implementing the changes that would sustain alumni-giving growth above and beyond the 30 percent participation rate.

The timing for a three-year strategic plan would coincide with the conclusion of the university's successful capital campaign and put the annual giving program in a good position to sustain the campaign's fund-raising momentum after it had ended. Having set out what it wanted to accomplish, USC set about examining what it would take to succeed.

A CRITICAL EXAMINATION—INSIDE AND OUT

Once you've identified what you're trying to accomplish, it is important to understand what's standing in your way. The obstacles can certainly be internal—whatever has caused you to fall short of your goals so far needs to be changed. In addition, plenty of external factors and forces can undermine the best-laid plans. The more research you perform to identify external trends and challenges, the more likely your strategic plan will succeed.

USC's annual giving people started by identifying the internal issues and trends that impacted its ability to achieve its identified goals. They evaluated data from the past several years—and also evaluated their ability to get data it would need in the future.

That's a critical point. Remember "the plural of anecdote is not data"? Unfortunately, too many annual giving decisions are based on a single angry phone call or similar anecdotal datum. If you are willing to settle for the few gift reports you can get out of your database or if surveying alumni is a luxurious non-option, at least realize that some of your decisions may be on less-than-firm ground. In my opinion, a strategic planning process is an opportunity to think about the data you need to accomplish your goals. As my friend and consulting colleague, William Lowery, is fond of saying, "We achieve what we measure."

WHAT'S GOING ON HERE?

In looking at some of the internal factors that were going to impact the annual giving program's ability to achieve its goals, USC identified the following issues:

- **Continually increasing new-donor-acquisition costs were impacting the program.** As a result of higher fund-raising appeal expenses that were yielding a lower percentage of responses, it was costing the annual giving program more and more money to attract fewer and fewer donors. Would the university need to explore other methods of conducting its appeals?

- **Inconsistent alumni-giving patterns, including a first-year donor retention rate that had decreased from more than 45 percent to less than 35 percent, meant that the donor base was very fragile.** Like the University of Michigan (see Chapter 8), USC was paying a lot to acquire new donors and then not retaining them. Staff also lamented the lack of a reunion giving program as a tool for increasing donor retention, reactivating lapsed donors, and increasing overall donor giving capacity.

- **A lack of internal identity had produced low campus awareness and growing campus competition.** Many departments within USC's advancement division did not understand the nature of the annual giving program's goals or why they were important. Outside the division, many campus units were attempting (often with dismal results) their own fund-raising appeals, putting them in competition with the central annual giving office—and each other.

- **A lack of external identity—and market research—left the annual giving program detached from USC alumni.** The annual giving staff knew that alumni had little awareness of the annual giving program, but they had no research specific to USC alumni. USC needed to understand more specifically how *its* alumni felt about the school, what they knew about giving opportunities, and how they made their giving decisions.

- **Little integration with the alumni relations office kept "friend raisers" and "fund raisers" following separate plans.** Although the annual giving program's success was due in part to ongoing alumni affinity, there was little interaction between the annual giving program and USC's alumni relations program. Both pursued program goals that were largely independent of each other.

- **A lack of communication with peer institutions resulted in a lack of comparative data.** USC had inadequate information on how its peers were performing according to comparable fund-raising measures. Neither did it know what successful methods and strategies its peers were using. USC had not established useful dialogues with other institutions that might have improved its own program.

- **Frequent turnover in annual giving program staff leadership further undermined program growth.** Due to a previous lack of adequate planning, the program went back to square one every time a director of annual giving departed.

WHAT'S GOING ON ELSEWHERE?

USC's internal analysis was accompanied with an external analysis as well. As the annual giving team searched for trends and issues that were going to impact the program, some of their external findings included:

- **Competition for gift dollars from other not-for-profit organizations was increasing.** USC was fighting more (and more sophisticated) not-for-profit organizations for its share of alumni charitable giving dollars. Was the university adequately making the case that it deserved their support?

- **The increased prominence of published university rankings was drawing attention to alumni-giving participation.** Since *U.S. News & World Report* and others calculated alumni-giving participation rates into their college rankings, the university needed to make alumni participation a priority. Given USC's relatively poor (compared to its peers) 20 percent alumni participation in previous years, the increased importance of university rankings added extra urgency to improving alumni participation. "I know many colleagues who don't agree that giving participation is an effective measurement of 'customer satisfaction' with the USC educational experience, but it lent additional urgency to our need to increase participation anyway," said Warwick.

- **Lifestyle changes were impacting the way USC engaged with alumni.** USC discerned alumni lifestyle trends that included the increasing tendency of people to stay at home and/or remain at home. Increased home access to entertainment (pay-per-view), communications (e-mail), and other services (Internet) prompted people to venture outside less often. In addition, the retail marketplace had taught alumni to expect more customization and personal service. Replacing its past emphasis on high-volume transactions and processes, the annual giving program would need to be more mindful of relationship-building in its appeals.

- **Technology was changing alumni banking and communication practices.** E-mail messages had already outnumbered the mail pieces handled daily by the U.S. Postal Service, while online banking and shopping, electronic funds transfer, and other new technologies were continuing to impact everyday life. USC alumni expected their alma mater to utilize the same technologies that they used in their daily lives.

"Obviously, the methods of communication were changing," said Warwick. "We felt that part of our decline was attributable to these changes, because of our failure to implement new methods to let our prospects hear from us. Also important were the conclusions that people were drawing. Because they expected us to be on the leading edge of technology in our educational programs, they assumed that our fund-raising programs would reflect that as well."

BRIDGING THE GAP BETWEEN ISSUES AND GOALS

To address those issues and trends, the USC annual giving staff identified four core competencies for the program:

- Marketing, advertising, and programming
- Research, technology, and the database
- Organization, staffing, and infrastructure
- Strategic alliances

These four areas provided a structure for addressing the observed trends while staff implemented and ultimately achieved the strategic plan's goals and objectives.

Marketing, advertising, and programming

New marketing goals for the annual giving program were seen as critical for success. "We thought that all nonprofits were becoming smarter in thinking through their marketing strategies, so our goal was to try and get ahead of the curve," said Houlihan. The marketing goals they identified included:

- **Consistent internal identity.** To effectively promote the case for support to prospect audiences and integrate external marketing efforts among campus offices, the program needed to solidify its identity internally. This would involve greater annual giving staff coordination of campus fund-raising activities and internal awareness-building of the program's goals and strategies. "Because we didn't have the prominence we needed, a lot of people had gotten into fund raising themselves. We wound up with competing departments and programs that were lowering our overall income. Annual giving needed to assert its identity and coordinate the activities," said Houlihan.

- **Consistent external identity.** With its internal ducks lining up in a row, the program then focused on new marketing strategies for its external audience. They created a new logo and approached the program like a classic marketing proposition. They also investigated the most cost-effective ways to maximize "exposures" of their themes and messages. The plan led to several innovations, such as including promotional statements with USC affinity credit cards, promotional announcements on the campus public radio station, and yearlong ad campaigns in campus publications. As with the internal scheduling goal, all annual giving fund-raising materials would now be coordinated through the annual giving office. "We didn't want each unit to lose its identity through this process, but we wanted to ensure that the USC annual giving program had a presence and an identity in all of the materials sent out," said Houlihan.

- **Continual market research.** The research conducted at the beginning of the strategic plan process taught staff that they needed to keep a finger on the pulse of their audience and to continually update their appeals.

Research, technology, and the database

The wave of new online communications dictated the prioritizing of technology upgrades and innovations. The staff made a commitment to improve the program's capabilities for communicating with alumni in new ways using the Internet, e-mail, Web sites, audio/video, and other media.

Organization, staffing, and infrastructure

Shifting communications preferences of alumni dictated structural changes to the annual giving program as well. Telemarketing and direct mail resources were repositioned to complement new online innovations. The USC annual giving program wanted to identify all alumni able to communicate via the Internet. This way, they could get to the point where they could reach prospects the way prospects preferred: by mail, phone, or computer.

Face-to-face contact was also reviewed. Increasing customer service expectations led to a reorganization that emphasized getting out of the office and meeting prospects in person. Houlihan shifted staff responsibilities to allow for additional personal solicitation activities, with many tied to alumni relations programs so as to leverage the goals of each.

Strategic Alliances

The strategic planning process yielded increased awareness of the strong relationship between effective alumni relations and annual giving programs. The annual giving program's strategic plan, as a result, established as a priority renewed collaboration and shared program goals between the two areas.

The plan has succeeded in providing a critical context for the program and a roadmap for its future. "It was an opportunity for continuity that just didn't exist before," said Houlihan, "and it's only the first strategic plan. This is the first step of a process that will keep the annual giving program moving forward for years to come."

McKENDREE COLLEGE: A PLAN FOR TODAY

For many schools, a worthwhile goal involves getting organized for *this* year. A multiyear strategic vision would be great, but first things first.

McKendree College in Lebanon, Illinois, follows a simple but effective annual giving operating plan format. It tells the reader about the program's recent history, outlines specific goals for the coming year, notes what activities will occur throughout the year, and details its budget needs. "Most people, especially board members, immediately flip through the plan to see the bottom line of our fund-raising projections," said Terry Andrews, the McKendree College director of annual giving. "We provide quantifiable monetary goals, but it's important for people to look at those numbers in the bigger context."

While not a full-blown strategic plan, McKendree's format reminds everyone about where the annual giving program is at. As Andrews said, "We look at what we're doing, where we've been, and where we're trying to go in the future."

THE McKENDREE COLLEGE ANNUAL GIVING ONE-YEAR OPERATING PLAN FORMAT

1. BACKGROUND

- BRIEF HISTORY OF PROGRAM
  What is the mission of the program?
  What has been the performance?
  What issues have impacted the
  program in the past?

- CURRENT SCOPE OF PROGRAM
  How is the program organized?
  How is the program staffed?
  What are the program's main activities?

2. THIS YEAR'S GOALS

- MONETARY GOALS
  What is overall dollar goal?
  What are goals for restricted and
  unrestricted gifts?

- NON-MONETARY GOALS
  What is the goal for alumni-giving
  participation?
  What else will we be trying to
  accomplish?

3. PLANS AND ACTIVITIES

- CONTINUING PROGRAMS
  What appeals will continue to occur
  this year?
  When and how will they happen?

- NEW PROGRAMS
  What new initiatives are we undertaking this year?
  How and when will they occur?

4. EVALUATION PLAN

- At what times during the course of
  the year will we measure and evaluate our progress toward the goals?

- What reports or other data will we
  need to monitor and evaluate our
  progress?

5. BUDGET REQUIREMENTS

- What funds are necessary to conduct
  the appeals we've outlined?

- What is the cost per appeal, and what
  is the projected cost per dollar raised
  for each?

- What is the total cost of the proposed
  annual giving program?

6. SUMMARY

- What concluding information does
  the reader need to know?

- Let's go!

About the Author

Robert A. Burdenski's travels as a consultant have made him a repository of annual giving ideas and best practices. He is a popular speaker and author whose work frequently appears in the CASE magazine, CURRENTS. *Innovations in Annual Giving: 10 Departures That Worked* is his first book.

Burdenski has spent more than 17 years in fund raising, serving a variety of educational institutions, as well as religious and human services organizations. Since 1994 he has served as a consultant in annual giving, alumni relations, and constituent market research for more than 100 colleges, universities, hospitals, and other types of not-for-profit institutions as a member of two long-time CASE affiliate firms— Grenzebach, Glier and Associates, and (since 1999) Bentz Whaley Flessner. His education clients have included the Stanford Business School, the University of California at Berkeley, New York University, Colorado College, Calvin College, the University of Michigan, the University of Bath (UK), and Wellesley College.

Burdenski's reach also extends to the Internet. Since 2001, he has served as the moderator of FundList (*www.fundlist.info*), the fund-raising profession's largest e-mail discussion group, with more than 2,000 active subscribers.

Prior to his consulting work, Burdenski served as director of annual giving and then director of university development at Cleveland State University, vice president for development at Catholic Charities Corporation in Cleveland, and chief development officer at Notre Dame College of Ohio. He is a graduate of Miami University in Oxford, OH.

Bibliography and Suggested Readings

Arneson, Karen W. "Discovering Alumni That Time Forgot: Under New Leadership, N.Y.U. Taps an Underused Resource," *New York Times*, November 16, 2002.

Bragg, Bob. "Seven Ideas for Highly Effective Fund Raising: To Achieve the Best Results From All Your Callers, Regardless of Their Skills, You Must Have an Effective Training Program and Motivational Reward System," *Fund Raising Management* 28, no. 2, April 1997.

Burdenski, Robert A. and Jeff Hauk. "Great Catches: Fish Through Your Database for New Annual Fund Prospect Segments," CURRENTS, April 1999.

Burdenski, Robert A. and Jeff Hauk. "Is Direct Mail Dead? Although Use May Be Waning, Direct Mail Is Still a Viable Fund-Raising Format. Here Are 10 Ways Campuses Are Breathing New Life Into the Medium," CURRENTS, October 1998.

Burdenski, Robert A. "Out of the Shadows: Annual Giving Gains More Respect as a Career Destination," CURRENTS, February 2003.

Burdenski, Robert A. "Proceed According to Plan: Why and How to Create a Strategic Plan for the Annual Fund," CURRENTS, May/June 2000.

Cardillo, Charlie. "The Unexamined Donor: For Better Planning and Greater Returns, Segment the Annual Fund by Giving Behavior," CURRENTS, May/June 2000.

Carlson, Mim. *Team Based Fundraising Step by Step: A Practical Guide to Improving Results Through Teamwork*. Jossey-Bass, 2000.

"The Charleston Principles: Regulating e-Philanthropy," *Nonprofit and Voluntary Sector Quarterly* 8, no. 1, April 2001.

Christ, Rick. "Put Your Direct Mail to the Test: Try Out New Annual-Fund Strategies—One at a Time—To Increase Your Returns With Less Risk," CURRENTS, May 1998.

Colson, Helen A. "Fund Raising at Independent Schools: The Challenges and the Assets," in *Handbook of Institutional Advancement*, 3rd ed. Council for Advancement and Support of Education, 2000.

Colson, Helen A. *Philanthropy at Independent Schools*. 2d ed. National Association of Independent Schools, 2002.

"Dealing With Objections: For Every Reason Not to Give, There's a More Compelling Reason To Give. Here's How to Turn Common Donor Objections Into Stronger Cases for Support," CURRENTS, April 1997.

Dickey, Marilyn. "E-Mailing for Dollars: Charities Use Electronic Messages to Reach Computer-Savvy Donors," *Chronicle of Philanthropy* 10, no. 22, September 10, 1998.

Dickey, Marilyn. "Free Money: How Charities Can Make the Most of Matching Gifts," *Chronicle of Philanthropy* 9, no. 10, March 6, 1997.

Dickey, Marilyn. "Rethinking Annual Campaigns: Charities Apply Same Techniques Used to Seek Big Gifts," *Chronicle of Philanthropy* 10, no. 12, April 9, 1998.

Dove, Kent E., Jeffery A. Lindauer & Carolyn P. Madvig. *Conducting A Successful Annual Giving Program: A Comprehensive Guide and Resource*. Jossey-Bass, 2001.

Gabrick, Andrea. "Playing Quarters: One Institution's Offbeat Fund-Raising Program Yields More Than Pocket Change," CURRENTS, January 2001.

Gardyn, Rebecca. "Generosity and Income: Wealth Isn't the Only Determining Factor in Whether a Person Volunteers or Gives to Charity," *American Demographics* 25, no. 1, December 2002/January 2003.

Gilbert, Michael C. "The E-mail Manifesto: It May Seem Mundane Compared With A Whiz-Bang Web Site, But E-mail Works," CURRENTS, January 2002.

Goldsmith, Richard. *Direct Mail for Dummies*. IDG Books Worldwide, 2000.

Hart, Ted. "The ePhilanthropy Revolution," *Fund Raising Management* 32, no. 3, May 2001.

Hedstrom, Elizabeth. "Testing Assumptions: One University's Challenge to Annual Giving Beliefs," CURRENTS, March 2001.

Heuermann, Robert. "A Higher Calling: Your Fund-Raising Efforts Are Crucial to the Future. Here's Why," CURRENTS, April 1997.

Heuermann, Robert. *It's Your Call: Training Tips and Techniques for Phonathon Callers*. Council for Advancement and Support of Education, reprinted from April 1997 CURRENTS.

Hodiak, Diane L. and John S. Ryan. *Hidden Assets: Revolutionize Your Development Program with a Volunteer-Driven Approach*. Jossey-Bass, 2001.

"How They Got The Gift: Penn Fund Raisers Land a $10 Million Gift Via E-Mail," *Chronicle of Higher Education*, February 18, 2000.

Hummerstone, Robert G. "World-Class Annual Funds: Here's How to Take Your Appeal Abroad to Tap Some of Your Best Prospects," CURRENTS, April 1998.

Independent Sector. *Giving in Tough Times: The Impact of Personal Economic Concerns on Giving and Volunteering*. Independent Sector, 2003.

"Integrating the Web, Email and Telemarketing: A Case Study," *Advancing Philanthropy*, May/June 2002.

Jackson, Laura Christion. "Outgrowing The Annual Fund: Keep the Largest Donors Happy With Special Cultivation, Solicitation, and Stewardship Techniques," CURRENTS, April 2001.

Johnston, Michael. "Fund Raising On the Net," in *The Nonprofit Handbook: Fund Raising*. Wiley, 2001.

Johnston, Michael. "The Internet and the Regulation of the Not-for-profit Sector," in *The Nonprofit Handbook: Fund Raising*. Wiley, 2001.

Johnston, Michael. *Direct Response Fund Raising: Mastering New Trends for Results*. Wiley, 2000.

Johnston, Michael. *The Fund Raiser's Guide to the Internet*. Wiley, 1999.

Lajoie, Scott. "Believe the Hype: Kansas State Doesn't Need to Pay Telefund Callers When It's Got Loyal Students," CURRENTS, April 2002.

Lajoie, Scott. "Plotting Online Gift Strategies," CURRENTS, April 2002.

Lewis, Nicole. "Fund-Raising Researchers Issue Guidelines Designed to Protect Privacy of Charity Donors," *Chronicle of Philanthropy*, February 8, 2001.

Lister, Gwyneth J. *Building Your Direct Mail Program*. Jossey-Bass, 2001.

Luan, Jing. "Data Mining and Its Applications in Higher Education," in *Knowledge Management: Building a Competitive Advantage in Higher Education: New Directions for Institutional Research*, no. 113. Jossey-Bass, 2002.

Lysakowski, Linda and Judith Snyder. "Fund Raising on Main Street: Local Business Support of Your Annual Fund Can Solidify Your Campus's Ties to Its Community," CURRENTS, January 2000.

"Making the Call: A Step-By-Step Guide from 'Hello' to 'Thank You, Goodbye'—And Everything in Between," CURRENTS, April 1997.

"Many Happy Returns: Boosting Phonathon Pledge Fulfillment," CURRENTS, July/August 2000.

McBee, Shar. *To Lead Is to Serve: How to Attract Volunteers and Keep Them*. Point of Light Foundation, 2002.

McCurley, Steve and Sue Vineyard. *Handling Problem Volunteers: Real Solutions*. Heritage Arts Publishing, 1998.

Metz, Amy Talbert. "Welcome to Camp Phonathon: Here's How to Transform Your Callers From Raw Recruits Into Polished Campus Ambassadors," CURRENTS, April 1997.

Myers, Tony and Guy Mallabone. "Significant Difference: Research Suggests Advancement Officers Should Pay Special Attention To Entrepreneurial Donors," CURRENTS, October 2001.

Patouillet, Leland D. "Alumni Association Members: Attitudes Toward University Life and Giving at a Public AAU Institution," *CASE International Journal of Educational Advancement* 2, no. 1 June 2001, Council for Advancement and Support of Education/Henry Stewart Publications.

Pearson, Jerold. "E-mail Newsletters and Institutional Advancement," *CASE International Journal of Educational Advancement* 2, no. 2, November 2001, Council for Advancement and Support of Education/Henry Stewart Publications.

Pearson, Jerold. "Many Happy Returns: Stanford University's Alumni E-newsletter Shows Positive Impacts On Campus Communications, Perceptions Of Alma Mater, and Alumni Giving," CURRENTS, May/June 2001.

"Phonathon Phollies: You'll Laugh, You'll Cry, You'll Motivate Your Callers by Relating These True Tales From the Trenches," CURRENTS, April 1997.

Pollack, Rachel H. "Divide and Conquer: Get More From Your Annual Fund by Targeting Appeals to Special Groups," CURRENTS, May 1998.

Pope, Tom. "Small Mailers: You Don't Need to Spend Millions," *NonProfit Times*, September 15, 2000.

Pope, Tom. "Special Report: Acquiring New Donors Comes From Testing," *NonProfit Times*, May 1997.

Price, Joyce Howard. "Census Data Show Drop-Off in Volunteerism," *Washington Times*, February 12, 2003.

Rieck, Dean. "Powerful Fund-Raising Letters—From A to Z: Part One of Three; Despite All the New Technology and Media We Have Available Today, the Letter Remains One of the Best Ways to Solicit Funds From a Wide Audience. It's Personal, Direct, and Cost-Effective," *Fund Raising Management* 29, no. 2, April 1998.

Rieck, Dean. "Powerful Fund-Raising Letters—From A to Z: Part Three of Three," *Fund Raising Management* 29, no. 4, June 1998.

Rieck, Dean. "Powerful Fund-Raising Letters—From A to Z: Part Two of Three," *Fund Raising Management* 29, no. 3, May 1998.

Roberts, Stevan, Michelle Feit, and Robert W. Bly. *Internet Direct Mail: The Complete Guide to Successful E-Mail Marketing Campaigns.* McGraw-Hill Trade, 2000.

Roth, Kimberlee. "Small Charities Find Online Giving Full of Rewards and Challenges," *Chronicle of Philanthropy*, October 23, 2002.

Roth, Kimberlee. "Tips for Creating an Online Fund-Raising System," *Chronicle of Philanthropy*, October 23, 2002.

Schaff, Terry and Doug. *The Fundraising Planner: A Working Model for Raising the Dollars You Need.* Jossey-Bass, 1999.

Schroeder, Fritz W. "Annual Giving: The Front Door to Your Development Program," in *Handbook of Institutional Advancement*, 3rd ed. Council for Advancement and Support of Education, 2000.

Schroeder, Fritz W. "Making Peace Between Annual and Major Gifts," CURRENTS, April 2001.

Schroeder, Fritz W. *Annual Giving: A Practical Approach.* Council for Advancement and Support of Education, 2000.

Schwartz, John. "After the Non-Revolution, Nonprofits Tiptoe Online," *New York Times*, November 18, 2002.

Seltzer, Michael. *Securing Your Organization's Future: A Complete Guide to Fundraising Strategies*, rev. ed. Foundation Center, 2001.

Sommerfeld, Meg. "One in Four Americans Volunteers, Report Says," *Chronicle of Philanthropy*, January 23, 2003.

Squires, Con. "Recapturing the Lapsed Perennial Donor, Part I," *Fund Raising Management* 28, no. 7, September 1997.

Squires, Con. "Recapturing the Lapsed Perennial Donor, Part II," *Fund Raising Management* 28, October 1997.

Squires, Con. "Renewing the First-Time Donor," *Fund Raising Management* 28, no. 4, June 1997.

Squires, Con. "Using Skillful Direct Mail Methods Towards Your Fund Raising Efforts," *Fund Raising Management* 28, no. 1, March 1997.

"Stamps May Boost Direct Mail Response," *Fund Raising Management* 27, no. 12, February 1997.

Stanczykiewicz, Bill. *Engaging Youth In Philanthropy*. Jossey-Bass, 2003.

Stein, Michael and John Kenyon. *The E-Nonprofit: A Guide to ASPs, Internet Services, and Online Software*. CompassPoint Nonprofit Services, 2002.

Stoner, Michael. "Managing Technological Change," in *Handbook of Institutional Advancement*, 3rd ed. Council for Advancement and Support of Education, 2000.

Taylor, Amy Jo. "Big Things From Small Packages: How to Motivate Student Callers in Tight Places on a Tight Budget," CURRENTS, May 1998.

"Tips for Calling Success: These Do's and Don'ts Will Keep Your Calls Running Smoothly," CURRENTS, April 1997.

Toppe, Christopher M., Arthur D. Kirsch, Jocabel Michel. *Independent Sector. Giving and Volunteering in the United States: Findings from a National Survey*. 2001 ed. Independent Sector Publications Center, 2002.

Toward, Christopher. "The Young and the Restless: Alumni in Their 20s, 30s, and 40s Can Be an Untapped Source of Major Gifts for Your Campus, but They May Not Sit Still for the Usual Appeals," CURRENTS, February 1999.

Walker, Mary Margaret. "Balancing Act: Managing Alumni Relations and the Annual Fund Is No Easy Feat. To Master the Art, Begin with These Five Lessons," CURRENTS, May 1997.

Walker, Theresa. "Calling All Student Volunteers: Campus Groups Earn Cash For Their Cause Through Phonathon Work," CURRENTS, September 2001.

Warwick, Mal. *The Five Strategies for Fundraising Success: A Mission-Based Guide to Achieving Your Goals*. Jossey-Bass, 2000.

Warwick, Mal. *How to Write Successful Fundraising Letters*. Jossey-Bass, 2001.

Warwick, Mal. *Testing, Testing 1, 2, 3: Raise More Money With Direct Mail Tests*. Jossey-Bass, 2003.

Warwick, Mal, Ted Hart, and Nick Allen. *Fundraising On The Internet: The ePhilanthropy Foundation.Org's Guide to Success Online.* Jossey-Bass, 2002.

Williams, Grant. "Guidelines Show Charities How to Work With Internet Companies on Fund Raising," *Chronicle of Philanthropy*, November 2, 2000.

Williams, Grant. "Web Issues and the IRS: A Hot Topic," *Chronicle of Philanthropy*, March 8, 2001.

Williams, Karla A. *Donor Focused Strategies for Annual Giving.* Aspen Publishers, July 1997.

Wylie, Peter B. "The Many Facets Of Data Mining: Fund-Raising Databases Are Filled With Gems If You Know How to Dig," CURRENTS, September 2001.

Wylie, Peter B. "Model Behavior: Statistical Modeling Can Help You Find the Right Equation for Annual Fund Success," CURRENTS, April 1999.

Index

stewardship, 51
  e-mail newsletters, 52
  strategies for, 85
strategic alliances, 119, 126
strategic planning, 116
  for annual giving, 7–8, 115–27
  rationale for, 117–20
student development: Junior Networking
  Night (Stanford), 58, 60
  opportunities for, 57–58
  sophomore academic dinners, 58, 60
  Stanford Fund Student Group
    Partnership, 59, 60
  Stanford University program, 55–62
student-driven phonathons, 113
  Freshman Thank-A-Thon (Stanford),
    57–58, 60
  Stanford Student Calling Program,
    58–59, 60
supports, 4
Sweet Briar College, 52
SYBUNTS (some years but not this year), 21

Target Analysis Group donorCentrics™
  reports, 19
Team Telefund, 33–37
technology, 119, 123, 125
telemarketing: Freshman Thank-A-Thon
  (Stanford), 57–58, 60
  K-State caller placemat, 34–35
  lessons, 40
  phonathons, 6, 52
  prizes for caller retention, 33
  Stanford Student Calling Program,
    58–59, 60
  student-driven phonathons, 113
  Team Telefund (K-State), 33–37
  volunteer, 6, 31–40, 52
themes, 24, 39
tracking data, 21
tradition, 37–38

UCLA Fund Web site, 52
University of California, Berkeley (UC
  Berkeley), 7, 108
  Cal Fund, 107–13
  dogs to alumni giving, 111, 112
  drivers for alumni giving, 111, 112
  hidden dogs to alumni giving, 111,
    112; location of, 6

University of California, Berkeley
  Foundation (UCBF), 108
University of California at Los Angeles
  (UCLA), 52
University of Durham, 52
University of Iowa (UI), 12
  direct mail program, 5, 11–23
  gift distribution, 21
  location of, 6
University of Iowa Foundation, 5, 11–23
University of Michigan (U-M), 7, 96
  data mining, 95–106
  First Time Donors (FTDs), 100
  location of, 6
  new-donor appreciation mailings, 97
  stewardship strategies, 85
  "Welcome Aboard" packages, 102, 103
University of Rochester, 42
  initial Internet strategy, 46–47
  location of, 6
  Parent Fund Web page, 45
  Rochester Fund, 41–52
  second Internet strategy, 48–49
  Young Alumni Giving Program, 46–47
University of Saskatchewan (U of S), 24–29
University of Southern California (USC), 116
  location of, 6
  strategic plan for annual giving, 7–8,
    115–27
University of Virginia (UVA): class giving,
  83–84
    reunion giving, 84
university rankings, 123
U.S. News & World Report, 123

video appeals, 52
Virginia Tech University, 106
volunteers, 38
  class agents, 76–78
  Exonian, 76–78, 80–82
  mobilizing, 82
  at Phillips Exeter Academy, 7, 73–84
  phonathons, 31–40
  prizes for, 33; training for, 78

Webcams, 40, 52
Web sites, 6, 22, 52
  annual giving, 52
  class Web pages, 52
  installment credit card pledges via, 52
  introducing, 100